DUBLIN'S OTHER POETRY
Rhymes and Songs of the City

JOHN WYSE JACKSON lives in County Wexford. Among his books are *John Stanislaus Joyce* (with Peter Costello), *We All Want to Change the World: A Life of John Lennon*, and *Dublin: Poetry of Place* (an anthology that is entirely different to this one).

HECTOR McDONNELL lives in County Antrim. One of Ireland's leading artists, he has written several books (*Ireland's Round Towers*, *The Wild Geese of the Antrim MacDonnells*, etc.) and illustrated others, such as *Diction Aires & French Letters* (by Elizabeth Wise), *Flann O'Brien at War* (edited by John Wyse Jackson) and a prize-winning edition of *The Night that Larry was Stretched*.

THE EDITORS have also worked together on *Ireland's Other Poetry: Anonymous to Zozimus* and *Ulster's Other Poetry: Verses and Songs of the Province*. If you know of any further examples of 'Other Poetry' that deserve to be rescued, they would be delighted to hear from you via the publisher or by email at irelandsotherpoetry@hotmail.com. Such discoveries feature on a web page, http://irelandsotherpoetry.spaces.live.com.

The book is dedicated, with love, to
Eoghan Mitchell and Rose McDonnell.

DUBLIN'S OTHER POETRY
Rhymes and Songs of the City

Edited by John Wyse Jackson
and Hector McDonnell

THE LILLIPUT PRESS
DUBLIN

First published 2009 by
THE LILLIPUT PRESS
62–63 Sitric Road, Arbour Hill
Dublin 7, Ireland
www.lilliputpress.ie

ISBN 978 1 84351 161 8

10 9 8 7 6 5 4 3 2 1

A CIP record for this title is available
from The British Library.

Set in 11.5 on 14pt Dante by Marsha Swan
Printed in England by MPG Books, Bodmin, Cornwall

Contents

(Verses are arranged alphabetically by author or, if anonymous, by title. Inverted commas denote working titles supplied for this edition.)

Rhymes and Reasons:
An Introduction

We are very happy indeed to present *Dublin's Other Poetry* to our ravenous readers. It is a sequel to our last volume, *Ireland's Other Poetry: Anonymous to Zozimus* (2007), an anthology of Irish humorous poetry which drew material from all corners of the island, as well as from four centuries of history. Inevitably, there were several poems and songs about Dublin in it, but we are particularly proud of the fact that we have found so much good material that none of the ones from the first volume is repeated here. We hope you will discover many new favourites as well as a few unexpected twists to some old friends among the verses we have chosen for this collection.

What on earth, you may reasonably ask, do we mean by 'Other Poetry'? The simplest answer is to suggest that you browse through the pages of this book. You will meet parodies, ballads, mock-heroic metrical narratives, bawdy odes, political and personal satires, unashamed doggerel, drinking songs, old-style light verse, comic recitations and even advertising copy for Dublin's most famous product, Guinness, in addition to a clutch of curiosities that defy categorization. Now and again you may even encounter the deep note of true poetry, but we trust that you will find that all the entries are resolutely unpretentious, and that they also share a common purpose – a belief that life may be quite good fun. You will also notice (we hope) that almost every entry here uses metre and rhyme.

'The troublesome and modern bondage of Rhyming,' wrote John Milton in his preface to *Paradise Lost*, is 'no necessary adjunct or true ornament of poem or good verse … but the invention of a barbarous age, to set off wretched matter and lame metre.' Poets of the modern age have tended to agree with him: no longer are they expected to upset the fluency of their minstrelsy by going through an agonizing search for a rhyme for 'silver' or 'orange'. Milton, however, would probably have been distressed to discover that most of today's poets have also ditched the old, highly skilled practice of metrical prosody. Sometimes, admittedly, this has been replaced by a loose, vaguely rhythmical beat, but many contemporary poems can be distinguished from some weird form of prose only by an extravagantly low ratio of words per page and a certain preciousness of diction. These days, the antiquated fripperies of rhyme and metre are generally reserved for less high-minded endeavours – in short, for exactly what we have christened 'Other Poetry'.

Happily Dublin has a long history of this sort of 'unserious' versemaking. The earliest poems in these pages come from the eighteenth century, the time of Jonathan Swift, Thomas Sheridan and their successors, who built up a lively habit of satirical verse. This form of educated satire ran in tandem with another, less polished, body of work by urban balladeers, dealing with city realities that were totally ignored by all other chroniclers, such as that anonymous sequence of macabre recitations of which the most famous is 'De Night before Larry was Stretch'd'.

Dublin's growing middle classes were soon adding new literary spices to this stew, and creating their own varieties of occasional verse, some of which even got into print. Various irreverent books such as *Pranceriana* and *The Parson's Horn-book* appeared, poking fun in mock-heroic couplets at any august figures that deserved derision, such as particularly pompous provosts of Trinity College or bishops of the Established Church. Convivial societies were founded which held regular meetings in town to 'quaff the flowing bowl' and exchange their latest poetic offerings. Needless to say these were not always of the highest quality. On top of these delights, in the early decades of the nineteenth century, periodicals came and went too, like *Grant's Almanack*, the *Comet*, *Paddy Kelly's Budget* and the *Dublin Satirist*. There you could catch up on the latest gossip and scandal and try to make sense of their riddles, rhymes and rebuses. Apparently readers were hugely tickled by these anonymous effusions, though not much in these journals seems likely to tickle anyone's fancy today, not even the contributions of a youthful James Clarence Mangan. Indeed, to modern eyes, most of the wit in these books and papers has quietly curled up and died, and so we have not burdened this collection with very much from them, entertaining though they must have seemed at the time.

There was however a much more creative printing industry operating in nineteenth century Dublin and catering for a mass public with less rarefied tastes. From the back rooms of bookshops and junkshops one-man presses poured forth a stream of crudely printed broadsheets bearing new and old songs, ballads and comic poems. This was the milieu of Dublin's most famous old ballad singer, Zozimus – a small selection of whose work rounds off this volume, as it did the last. Cheap pamphlets were also churned out with the lyrics of the latest hits of the season, as performed on stage at variety shows in the Theatre Royal and elsewhere. Many of these songs and recitations were English imports, but Dublin compositions were equally popular, including the anonymous 'Stoney Pocket's Auction', a ballad that itself explores this alternative Irish mythopoeia of song. (It may be found below on page 115.)

As time went by, and the habit of reading spread, the second half of the nineteenth century saw a succession of comic magazines in Dublin – *Pat's Paper*, *Zozimus* and a dozen others. Usually written by small groups of like-minded friends, few of them lasted long, but they often contained witty excursions in verse, offering rare insights into changing moods in the Irish capital during the half-century that led up to independence. Just about the last magazine in that mould was *Dublin Opinion*, which began with the foundation of the state in 1922, and it was by far the best of the lot. Some verses from that paper appear in *Ireland's Other Poetry*, and a couple more have found their way into this volume too, as well as some spirited examples from some of its Victorian predecessors.

During the twentieth century, several writers, both amateur and professional, have found outlets for their 'Other Poetry'. During the 1920s, for instance, George Bonass, a career civil servant, was given a regular spot for his occasional verse in the *Dublin Evening Mail*, while the journalist M.J. MacManus had various collections of his rhymes and parodies published in book form. At both Trinity College and University College, Dublin, undergraduates contributed verses to student magazines, and *TCD Miscellany* in particular was so productive that a book of the best of it was issued in 1945, and sold well. Several of these student scribblers later became celebrated for quite different achievements, including the late Conor Cruise O'Brien. He had copious quantities of light verse published in *TCD Miscellany*, but it was all so topically allusive that only detailed annotations would make it comprehensible today, and in the process half the fun would melt away. So, alas, nothing by the Cruiser appears here. Happily, however, the book opens with a *TCD* poem by one of his near contemporaries, Fergus Allen, now one of our most admired 'proper' poets.

Chance has played a large part in the survival of certain strands of 'Dublin's Other Poetry', such as the off-colour verses that have always circulated by word of mouth through the city. The ruderies of Oliver St John Gogarty were eventually collected in book form, and so too were Daragh Smith's almost legendary 'medical verses' (two of which are in this collection), but it is now very difficult to locate other similarly ephemeral verses, many of which may not even have been written down. The following snatch of Dublin ribaldry, for example, would almost certainly have been lost to posterity if James Joyce hadn't put it into *Ulysses*, where Molly Bloom remembers hearing some lads chanting it one day at the corner of Marrowbone Lane. It is of course a riddle, about repairing a sweeping-brush:

My Uncle John
Has a thing long,
My Aunt Mary
Has a thing hairy,
And he puts his thing long
Into my Aunt Mary's
Hairy ...

On the flyleaf of *Ireland's Other Poetry* we asked readers to tell us about any further interesting verses, ephemeral or otherwise, that they felt we ought to have put in the book. We are grateful to the many kind people who sent us suggestions (including, in some cases, their own compositions). Several of these discoveries appear in this volume, and more may be read on a webpage that we set up for the purpose, which can be visited at http://irelandsotherpoetry.spaces.live.com. If you know of anything good that we may have overlooked, we would still be delighted to hear from you by email at irelandsotherpoetry@hotmail.com.

Gathering and organizing material for this book has once again been a very happy task for both editors. Hector has enjoyed making his drawings to illuminate the verses, and John has enjoyed looking at them. When the previous volume appeared, one reviewer was disappointed that we hadn't included an essay tracing the origins and history of 'Ireland's Other Poetry'. You won't find one in this book either, so we will all have to wait until a full academic treatment of the subject is eventually written by somebody else. In the meantime, if you are pining for literary history, we have tried to supply in the headnotes a little more information about the poets and their work than we did in the first book. As before, the entries are arranged alphabetically by author, or by title where the author is unknown to us, and there is an index of titles and first lines at the back of the book.

John Wyse Jackson
Hector McDonnell

DUBLIN'S OTHER POETRY

Fergus Allen

What we mean by 'Other Poetry' remains something of a movable feast, but one branch of it is certainly light verse. Lately this has fallen into disrepute, perhaps because too often it degenerates into throwaway doggerel. But along with wit, successful light verse demands a high degree of technical skill as well. The real powerhouse of this sort of poetry in twentieth-century Ireland was Trinity College Dublin, so it is pleasing that we can begin our alphabet with an excellent example from TCD Miscellany in the 1940s. The decade was probably the light-verse heyday of that most exceptional undergraduate magazine.

Fergus Allen (b. 1921) is far more than a composer of light verse, of course. As a prizewinning 'proper poet' he has issued four fine collections of his work in the last two decades, and we are duly grateful to him for allowing us to pluck this apprentice piece from obscurity.

The verses were an ironic reply to a recent article in the paper about Trinity's place in modern Ireland:

> *It is not, to be sure, easy to change a tradition that has run in a single groove for centuries … It is well to be reminded once in a while that T.C.D. possesses a Gaelic Society … Trinity can, if it rids itself of ancient prejudices and outworn ideas, play no small part in this great national work.*
>
> *– Irish Press, November 23, 1943.*

TO TRINITY COLLEGE, 1943

Four hundred years have well-nigh passed,
The shades of night are falling fast,
Can aught avail our noble caste,
My Trinity?

This place where Art and Science wed,
Where scholars stalk and angels tread

3

And join to praise the mighty dead
Of Trinity!

Where shapes of things to come are shaped,
Where locks are neither picked nor raped—
The Gaelic League has got us taped,
My Trinity!

They soon will come, a Celtic rout,
Athirst for blood, incensed with stout,
To throw our foreign culture out,
My Trinity!

Is this the working of the curse,
Is this the Anglo-Irish hearse,
To hear the natives speaking Erse
In Trinity?

With curling lip and scornful eye
We hear the Gaelic hue and cry,
We watch the peasants passing by,
From Trinity!

Our sneer of cold command still quells,
We've got the savoir-vivre that tells,
We've got the blasted Book of Kells,
In Trinity!

Spirit of Cromwell! Rise again
And subjugate by sword or pen
These rude, uncouth, untutored men
To Trinity!

Peter Allt

Behind these atmospheric lines lurks Molière's play, Les Precièuses Ridi-cules, *a satire on Mme Rambouillet's 'salon bleu' in early seventeenth-century Paris. When the elegant and gifted Peter Allt (1917–54) wrote them in the late 1930s, he still had his major work on Yeats's poetry ahead of him, but would already have been quite a catch for any of Dublin's literary 'at-homes'. Quite an aesthete himself, Allt had a provocative turn of phrase – he once compared Patrick Kavanagh and other 'revolutionary' Irish poets like him to 'coal-heavers at a sherry party'. He died tragically young, in a railway accident.*

POEM

Ghost of a ghost of Madame Rambouillet
Presiding like a blanket in the room,
My wings well clipped; tongue clipped; perforced to stay
I smile like one who has foreseen his doom,
Or a cynic faute de mieux accepts a destined tomb.

My lady hostess polymath advances
(On charm and sausages her poets fed),
Sidles, with twisted neck, and sidelong glances
'And what is it you do, my dear?' I shake a
golden head
Glumly; and wonder why the paths of glory
Lead (so monotonously) to a double-bed.

Scented, tattooed, and clad in velvet breeches
I am engulfed with Baudelaires and
Nietzsches.
Sandals and sweaters, purple shirts, green bows,
Marlowes pursue me, Michelangelos.

Anonymous

The nineteenth century saw many periodicals come and go in Dublin. Ireland's Other Poetry *(this book's predecessor) found several good verses in Richard Dowling's light satirical magazine of the early 1870s,* Zozimus *– named after the Dublin balladeer who became our book's patron saint.*

Ten years later, Zozimus *had folded, but a similar humorous journal,* Pat's Komik, *usually known simply as* Pat, *was being produced by W.P. Swan 'at the Carlton Steam Printing Works, 9 William Street'. There, the resident poet (or band of poets – contributors were strictly anonymous) presented an occasional series of lively odes, called 'Lyra Liffeiana', about celebrated spots in and around the city. Some of the best (or oddest) of them are reprinted in this volume. This one, a frothy, briny confection about the popular northside resort of Balbriggan, appeared in* Pat on *9 September 1882.*

BALBRIGGAN:
AT THE LADIES' BATHING PLACE

By this town so famed for hoses,
Where the seaweed thickly growses,
Summer zephyrs softly blowses,
Yachts with sails as white as snowses,
Or at anchor safe reposes,
Fishing smacks as black as crowses,
Or little pigs with trichinosis
(Not the nasty smacks you knowses,
That elicit cries of woeses,
When they tingle on elbowses),
But the sort we sometimes rowses,
Where the tide it ebbs and flowses,
Right upon your back you goeses,
Nothing seen but knees and noses,

And ten funny little toeses,
Fishes flat with eyes like sloeses,
Blush as rubies red or roses,
Saying 'Oh! what shocking showses!'
Vulgar crabs cry 'Hokey Moses,
Where in goodness are their clotheses?'

Brendan Behan

Brendan Behan (1923–64) set little store by literary copyright, at least where others were concerned. His memory, under siege though it often was, retained countless verses and songs from many sources. Some of these he adapted for recycling in the normal literary way, but more often he changed them spontaneously during performance. The suspicion remains, therefore, that he was not in fact the originator of the song below; however he was certainly the one who made it familiar: his best play, The Quare Fellow, *can hardly be imagined without it.*

THE OLD TRIANGLE

A hungry feeling
Came o'er me stealing
And the mice were squealing in my prison cell,
And that old triangle
Went jingle jangle
Along the banks of the Royal Canal.

To begin the morning
The warder bawling
'Get out of bed and clean out your cell,'
And that old triangle
Went jingle jangle
Along the banks of the Royal Canal.

On a fine spring evening,
The lag lay dreaming
The seagulls wheeling high above the wall
And that old triangle
Went jingle jangle
Along the banks of the Royal Canal.

The screw was peeping
The lag was sleeping,
While he lay weeping for the girl Sal
And that old triangle
Went jingle jangle
Along the banks of the Royal Canal.

The wind was rising,
And the day declining
As I lay pining in my prison cell
And that old triangle
Went jingle jangle
Along the banks of the Royal Canal.

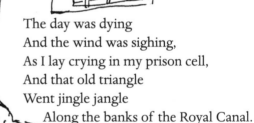

The day was dying
And the wind was sighing,
As I lay crying in my prison cell,
And that old triangle
Went jingle jangle
　　Along the banks of the Royal Canal.

In the female prison
There are seventy women
I wish it was with them that I did dwell,
Then that old triangle
Could jingle jangle
Along the banks of the Royal Canal.

George Bonass

George Bonass (1884–1942) was called to the Bar in 1908, thereafter becoming a lifelong civil servant. Civil servants who wrote were not advised to use their own names, and so he used the initials 'P.O.P.' for the many topical verses he contributed to the Dublin Evening Mail *in the 1920s. Cricket was another of his passions – he would eventually be elected President of the Irish Cricket Union – and he was the originator and organizer of the Phoenix Park 'Cab Derby', a race-cum-parade of Dublin horse-drawn cabs held on the last day of each year through the 1930s and into the '40s.*

In 1926 John Logie Baird had first demonstrated to a select group of interested scientists his work on 'seeing by wireless': the lines below, from Verse and Worse *(1928), a collection of P.O.P.'s best work, must be one of the earliest appearances of television in verse. As a prophet, George Bonass was up there with the best of them.*

A BALLADE OF THE FUTURE

Television has come to stay—
    Publish the tidings from shore to shore—
The darksome night has been turned to day,
    Nothing is hidden, for evermore.
If at a game of cards you'd play—
    Bridge or Poker appeal, no doubt—
Who holds aces, and who holds four?
    Look in your set, and you'll soon find out.

What is the Grocer doing, pray,
    Covertly there in his soft goods store?
Sand in the sugar! And we've to pay;
    Aye, but we'll swiftly settle his score.
Look at the Publican, watch him pour
    'Plain' in the 'Double,' and name it Stout;

Never again shall we cross his door;
    Look in your set, and you'll soon find out.

Where is your Maiden, winsome, gay,
    She who was true to you when on shore?
Who is she talking to? Who's the jay
    Holding her hand? Don't you want his gore
Staining the carpet, and couch, and floor?
    Is he a lover, or is he a lout?
Is he beloved, or just a bore?
    Look in your set, and you'll soon find out.

L'ENVOI

Things are altered from heretofore.
    If you are anxious at all about
What's going on in the house next door,
    Look in your set, and you'll soon find out.

*The abovementioned Publican's 'Plain' and 'Double' are the two grades of
Guinness that poured out of the St James's Gate brewery when these verses
were being written: Single X, 'plain' porter was weaker – and cheaper – than
the Double 'XX' stout we drink today. During the quarter of a millennium
since the first pint of Guinness was brewed, it inspired many poetical com-
positions. The one below was found in a 1961 issue of the company's in-house
magazine,* The Harp; *some four decades earlier it had probably been one of
the writer's* Evening Mail *contributions. The phenomenon mentioned in the
last line can be observed if you look through your pint at a bright light.*

A STOUT SAINT

Saint James he was a sturdy saint,
A sturdy saint was he,
He left a name that has wide-world fame
To a parish by Liffey free.
They built a Gate to this cleric great,
Where the river runs to the sea:
And his name is known in each Burgh and Town
And in every hostelrie.

Aye, it's travelled over the
    Seven Seas;
It's blessed in the tropic night,
Where men go out, brave
    men and stout,
To fight e'er the dawn be
    bright.
In Greenland's hills it cures
    most ills;
It saves the Igloo's plight;
And the midnight sun has
    nothing on
The gleam of the ruby light.

Vincent Caprani

The writer and printer, Vincent Caprani, is pickled in Dublin lore. His 1986 book, A View from the DART, *for example, explores the unsuspected delights that flank the main commuter line between Bray and Howth. The lines below takes a similar whistle-stop trip through the city's history. They come from* Rowdy Rhymes and Rec-im-itations: Doggerel for a Departed Dublin *(1982) – a now elusive collection of Caprani's verses. There, he supplies enjoyably scholarly notes about many of the figures mentioned here. For the young musician who has an honoured place at the end of this poem, for example, the entry reads:*

> *Bugler Dunne: The 15–year-old boy hero of the Boer war. During the crossing of the Tugela river in December 1899, and in the confusion caused by a surprise attack by the Boers, what might have been a disastrous rout for the British forces was turned into a partial victory by the bugler soundng 'Advance' instead of 'Retreat', as he had been instructed to do. When questioned later by superior officers the boy naively stated that, as it was his very first time under fire, he naturally took the order to be one of 'Advance' because his father (a career soldier and a sergeant in the Dublin Fusiliers) had always told him that the 'Fusiliers never retreat'.*
>
> *Dunne was later decorated, received at Buckingham Palace by the aging Queen Victoria, and then toured the British music halls with his 'bugle act' as part of a British army recruitment campaign. He served again in the Great War, was later a seaman, and died in his native Dublin in the 1950s.*

THE DUBLINER

I'm yo'r true-born native Dublin man – not aisy to define,
Save to say, in a prideful way, that I'm from ancient line.
I boast a noble lineage – I know it off by heart!—
Sir Tristan and Isolde, and Conor King MacArt.
For I'm Gael and Norse and Norman stock, and Huguenot moreover;
I'm Sitric blonde and Strongbow brave, and scion of Danish rover.

I'm Palatine (came from the Rhine), I'm Fleming and Walloon;
I'm soldier, sailor, jarvey, tailor; I'm pikeman and dragoon.
I'm weaver from the Liberties, a sawyer from Portobell-a,
I'm a butcher boy from Ormond quay, I'm a rag-and-bones 'oul fel-
    lah';
I'm the olive-skinned Eye-talian man that invented 'wan-and-wan'
Or hawked his holy ros'y beads from dawn 'till setting sun.
I'm Tiger Roche and Zozimus, I'm Billy-in-the-bowl;
I'm *pinkadindie, latchiko* – and the true 'heart of the rowel'.
I'm 'relationed' to the Twangman's mot, I've cousins one and all
That drank their fill at Finnegan's Wake, likewise the Ragman's Ball.
I've trawled for herrings in the bay, and sold them from a cart,
I've kissed the hand of Moll Malone, but couldn't win her heart.
I'm also kin to Skin-the-Goat that spurned the Saxon shillin'
(Could not be bought, donned convict cloth, before he'd act the
    villain!).

From Waterloo to 'Bastapol I've charged the foreign snipers
And left me blood on distant soil from Colenso down to 'Wypers';
At Easter Week I reached me peak, in my own native town
Though cannon blazed it took five days before they wore us down!
Thus Fusilier or Volunteer as the mood or memory rouses—
Yet a peaceable lar that likes a jar (so a curse on both their houses!)
And I've drawn the dole, and hefted coal with Whacker, Jem and Ned
And I've carried hods and stacked the sods upon the Featherbed.
From Ray-town out to Ballybough, and 'tween the two canals,
I've worked and toiled, I've kipped and moiled, with staunch and
    loyal pals.
From Harold's Cross I've pitched and tossed to Alexander's Basin
From day to day I've earned me pay with docker and with mason.
From Brazen Head to Monto town my wheel turns on its hub
And I draw my pride from Liffey side because I am a Dub!
So when the Judgement day is nigh, and I slip this mortal coil
No Gabriel's horn will sound that morn to salute my days of toil
No angels' choir will thus inspire, or sing my race is run
'Cause I'll proudly wait at the pearly gate for a 'toot' from the
    'Bugler' Dunne!

One night in July 1957, the equestrian statue of Field-Marshal Sir Hubert Gough in the Phoenix Park was dynamited. A few days later an anonymous broadsheet appeared, bearing these verses.

It was widely believed that they had been written by Brendan Behan (and we suggested as much in the first edition of Ireland's Other Poetry), *but in fact it was Vincent Caprani who dashed them off after the explosion. He would later admit the fact, 'with neither pride nor penitence', in* Rowdy Rhymes and Rec-im-itations.

GOUGH'S STATUE

There are strange things done from twelve to one
In the Hollow at Phaynix Park,
There's maidens mobbed and gentlemen robbed
In the bushes after dark;
But the strangest of all within human recall
Concerns the statue of Gough,
'Twas a terrible fact, and a most wicked act,
For his bollix they tried to blow off!

'Neath the horse's big prick a dynamite stick
Some gallant 'hayro' did place,
For the cause of our land, with a match in his hand
Bravely the foe he did face;
Then without showing fear – and standing well clear—
He expected to blow up the pair
But he nearly went crackers, all he got was the knackers
And he made the poor stallion a mare!

For his tactics were wrong, and the prick
    was too long
(The horse being more than a foal),
It would answer him better, this dynamite setter,
The stick to shove up his own hole!
For this is the way our
    'hayroes' today
Are challenging England's might,
With a stab in the back
    and a midnight attack
On a horse that can't even shite!

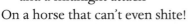

Anonymous

The second of our 'Lyra Liffeiana' from Pat *(17 September 1881). This strange ditty, with its unusual verse form, is as liquid as the first. 'Choriambics' are an extreme challenge to a poet's ingenuity, and are rarely encountered. Each of the lines here contains three metrical feet of four syllables, which have emphasis placed on the first and the last (as in 'stealing a kiss' or 'carcases cold').*

A year after this poem appeared, Carlisle Bridge would become O'Connell Bridge to mark the unveiling of J.H. Foley's statue of 'Great Dan'.

CHORIAMBICS FROM CARLISLE BRIDGE

Odoriferous stream, flowing to meet, sadly pollute the sea,
Flow, flow whither you please – flow
    to the deuce, only away from me.

    Wondrous children of deep, denizens
      dark, carcasses cold canine,
    Feline, sad-smelling forms, flow with
      the stream, flow to the azure brine;

There where congers around smilingly sit watching the finsome bride,
Whose king-consort august, lilting a lay, laudeth her lily side;

Where fair cockles around stealing a kiss mix with the mack'rel shoal,
Where blithe oysters, that cost nothing per doz., love to be eaten
    whole;

When there, sad-smelling forms, see that ye be pickled and purified,
Then back hie unto to me, hie with the sweet songs of those realms
    of pride—

Hie back, back to your homes, back to your maids, back to your
    heroes true,
Also kindly procure each one for me oysters a score or two.

Maurice James Craig

Maurice Craig was born in Belfast in 1919, and has lived in Dublin for many years. Now best known for innovative books of architectural history (notably Dublin 1660–1860*), in 1990 he defied fashion with* The Elephant and the Polish Question, *a volume of what might be called 'belles-lettres'. This nutritive gathering of his thoughts and observations vibrates with fun and wisdom: copies are hard to find, but if you track one down it will repay whatever you are charged for it.*

Craig's poems were published early. The one below, from Some Way for Reason *(1948), looks at Dublin as it was during World War II, when neutrality briefly redefined the Irish capital as a centre of high living – if only in comparison to the rest of blacked-out Europe.*

KILCARTY TO DUBLIN

The paraffin-lamps and the home-cured bacon
The whitewash misty behind the trees
Are taken apart and sorted and shaken
By a war that rages between the seas.
The sweets in the dim shop-window glitter
The idiot-girl still sniffs in the 'bus;
The literal meaning of all grows bitter
If not for her, then at least for us.
But life goes on in the last lit city
Just in the way it has always done
And pity is lost on the tongues of the witty
And the wolf at the door is a figure of fun.

John Philpot Curran

As a student at Trinity College Dublin, John Philpot Curran (1750–1817) was notably dissolute. In later life, the eminent barrister and orator never quite cleaned up his act. In 1779 he became 'Prior' of a political dining and drinking society called the Order of St Patrick, whose members were known as the 'Monks of the Screw' – the 'screw' in question being, naturally, a corkscrew. Curran's conversation at their meetings was reputedly so witty that 'the servants were frequently incapacitated from attending to the guests by laughter'. He was pleased to discover that the title allowed him to bluff his way into the winecellars of French monasteries – despite looking, as a contemporary put it, 'like the devil with his tail cut off'.

If, as Curran once argued, the brethren of other orders might be more celebrated for learning how to die, then the 'Monks of the Screw' were unsurpassed for knowing how to live. Here is the 'charter-song' he wrote for them – in verse three the 'lean face' he mentions is his own.

THE MONKS OF THE SCREW

When Saint Patrick this order established,
  He called us the 'Monks of the Screw';
Good Rules he revealed to our Abbot
  To guide us in what we should do;
But first he replenished our fountain
  With liquor the best in the sky;
And he said, on the word of a saint,
  That the fountain should never run dry.

Each year, when your octaves approach,
  In full chapter convened let me find you;
And when to the Convent you come,
  Leave your favourite temptation behind you.

And be not a glass in your Convent,
　　Unless on a festival found;
And, this rule to enforce, I ordain it
　　One festival all the year round.

My brethren, be chaste, till you're tempted;
　　While sober, be grave and discreet;
And humble your bodies with fasting,
　　As oft as you've nothing to eat.
Yet, in honour of fasting, one lean face
　　Among you I'd always require;
If the Abbot should please, he may wear it,
　　If not, let it come to the Prior.

Come, let each take his chalice, my brethren,
　　And with due devotion prepare,
With hands and with voices uplifted,
　　Our hymn to conclude with a prayer.
May this chapter oft joyously meet,
　　And this gladsome libation renew,
To the Saint, and the Founder, and Abbot,
　　And Prior, and Monks of the Screw!

Leslie Daiken

In both A Portrait of the Artist as a Young Man *and* Ulysses, *James Joyce refers to Ireland as 'the old sow that eats her farrow'. When he was living in Paris, he generally welcomed visitors from Dublin, and in October 1937, the socialist activist, anthologist and poet Leslie Daiken (1912–64) visited his flat at 7 rue Edmond Valentin. Sharing the novelist's jaundiced view of modern Ireland, Daiken afterwards wrote this quatrain as a message of solidarity from those who followed in Joyce's footsteps. It was published in 1944 in his first collection of poems,* Signatures of All Things – *another quotation from* Ulysses.*

LES JEUNES À JAMES JOYCE

We'd place in Dublin a carved monument
In Connemara marble telling how
Your fine infanticidal sow
Was most expressive of her temperament.

Morgan Dockrell

No longer can it be said, as it once used to be, that the best English is spoken in Dublin. Ireland's acknowledged doyen of verse about cricket, Morgan Dockrell (b. 1939) also finds time to focus his sharp eyes (and ears) on the ebb and flow of Dublin demographics. This satire packs a depth-charge in the eighth line: the plague of pretension that blights the speech patterns of South Dublin may often be a simple matter of emphasis.

AWKCENTS

Dolores Mac Aonghusa preens
Herself on living in RAWTHMEENS,
While Niamh Ní Dhomnaill's spirits soar
At having made it to RAWTHGAWR,
And Craoine Cailleach's constant squawk
Consists of cousins in FAWKSWRAWK.

These well-to-do up-market places
Encourage errors in ... emphasis
From those who posture at being 'posh',
But just succeed in talking tosh ...
Which goes to show – PRONUNCIATION
UNERRINGLY BETRAYS ONE'S STATION.

Anonymous

Generations of Dubliners have done their courting on the beaches of north and south Dublin. This entertaining song, sent to us by a kind reader of Ireland's Other Poetry, *takes its cue from Dominic Behan's hit, 'The Sea Around Us' – the lyrics of which appear in that book.*

DOLLYMOUNT STRAND

On Dollymount Strand on a cold winter's night,
I put on the hand brake and switched out the light.
I looked at me mot and said, 'Aye, are you right?'—
Meself and the architect's daughter.

Chorus:
But the sea, oh the sea, it crept up on me,
And the water was risin' up quite rapidly;
I sez to the mot, 'Get your hand off me knee.
Can't you see we're surrounded by water?'

I switched on the ignition and put it in gear.
Could I get it movin', lads? No, not a fear,
Not if I was there for the next bloody year—
There was sand in the old carburettor.

With water the car soon filled to the brim.
I sez to the mot, 'Dear, the chances are slim.
So, love, get them off here, we'll both have to swim.'
So I let down the window and scarpered.

So if ever you're down to Dollymount Strand
Be sure that the tide's out and everything's grand
For a bird in the bush is worth two in the hand—
Regardless of what you are after.

Anonymous

In 1790, Exshaw's Gentleman's and London Magazine (which was printed in Dublin) unveiled what it called 'a curious Grub-street ode on that celebrated nuisance Donnybrook Fair'. This detailed catalogue of those who attended the world-famous carnival-cum-market is unique. During the preparation of these modest headnotes, it was gratifying to see 'Annotators' listed among the other cheats, ruffians and obsessives who were there.

After a preamble calling for urgent assistance from Apollo, the god of poetry, the poet begins in earnest:

from DONNYBROOK FAIR: AN IRREGULAR ODE

Behold, what crowds at Donnybrook are seen,
Some clad in yellow, others dress'd in green!
Chimney-sweepers;
Brothel keepers;
Boys in rags;
Swarthy hags;
Buckish wags,
Who ride their nags;
Girls in tatters;
Wives in shatters;
Hosiers, hatters,
Mending matters;
Cheating bakers;

Pulpit shakers;
Money stakers;
Mantua-makers;
Drunken sailors;
Valiant tailors;
Undertakers;

27

Sabbath breakers,
(God's forsakers);
Midnight wakers;
Thieves, thief-takers,
Darting along, as if on wings they flew,
While harlots close the train, with eyelids black and blue!—
    But hark! what strains inspire these jovial souls!
    The piercing trumpet makes its voice to soar;
    And now the drum its martial thunder rolls,
    While prentice-boys robellow to the roar,
While drunkards, strumpets, thieves cry, *D—n your eyes —encore!*
    Behold the plenteous scene below,
    How clear and turfy embers glow;
And the fair cooks, establish'd on the town,
With nostrils dripping snuff, each luscious bit embrown:
And voices roar, 'Come here, and find relief,
Come here and regale with fat *Spoleens of Beef!*'

Carmen, tinkers,
Blind Free-thinkers;
Grunting Quakers,
Kennel-rakers;
Nymphs from stews;
Jabbering Jews;
Antiquarians;
Stubborn Arians;
Unitarians;
Presbyterians;
'Destinarians;
Apollonians;
Antimonians;
Muggletonians;
Sandemonians;
Purgatorians;
Fam'd chirurgeons;

Swedenbourgians;
Methodists,
With double fists;
Babes of grace
Who deal in lace;
Drunken peers;
Auctioneers;
Famous fighters;
Base back-biters.
Swift lamp-lighters;
Hackney writers;
Little bards,
Who're big blackguards;

Paltry play'rs,
And whores in pairs;
Thieving waiters;
Annotators;
Club-debaters,
Calculators;
Aged preachers,
Tumult teachers;
Attorneys' clerks,
Fine hopeful sparks;
Jack-ass drivers;
Pocket divers!

With numbers of those rhapsody enditers,
Those famous quill-men, call'd news-writers;
While Hate and Scandal as their Heralds fly,
To beg them bread – or else, the devils die,
All, all are here, to bless their happy stars,
And view, with rapt'rous eyes, this Champ de Mars!

M.F. Egan, SJ

For generations, Kingsbridge Railway Station (now patriotically known as Heuston Train Station) has been the starting-point for a million thrilling journeys south and west from the capital, but not many can have been as curious as this one. Described as a 'Period Piece', this poem was found in a very spirited book of verses, Ballads of Distraction and Other Poems *(1956), written by the Rev. Michael F. Egan, SJ (1876–1961). Fr Egan, a Cork-man, was not merely one of the small army of Irish literary Jesuits, he was also a distinguished mathematician, rising to Professor of Mathematics in University College, Dublin.*

MYSTIC JOURNEY

At Kingsbridge, whose thin and eager ridge
Is loving and bitter as a world-weary midge,
I got into the green-pink worried train,
Got out of it again and in again,
Was borne in its circumambient pain,
Across the murmuring indigo-orange plain
Through honeyed discords of the ebony rain,
Until I came, O Lord!
To infinite transparent Waterford,
A river tied to the end of a board,
River of tinkling treacle-beetles, poured
Over the exultant and despairing sward.

There, plangent odours from the Apennines
Were whispering amber sins, linnet-voiced pines
Carrying passionate clothes-lines,
Crooning a tune to the blue blue moon,
To the blue moon that whines

And moans and screeches along the far star-reaches,
Whines and shines and repines
For a world-weary midge
Lost on the fiery ridge
Of Kingsbridge.

Anonymous

Lines from a full-page illustrated advertisement for Guinness, in the January–February 1939 issue of National Student, *the undergraduate magazine of University College, Dublin. These unsigned and somewhat Bellocose verses may have been the work of the regular Guinness versifiers, Ronald Barton and Robert Benson.*

ENQUIRING EDWARD
AN INSTRUCTIVE TALE

Young Edward Egge, as we shall find,
Possessed a most enquiring mind;
He had a sort of natural bent
For what is called Experiment.

For instance, when he fell downstairs,
Although in need of some repairs,
He said he did not mind at all
Because this rather nasty fall
Provided striking confirmation
Of Newton's Law of Gravitation.

So when he heard some people say
(As people do from day to day)
'There's nothing like a Guinness', Ned
Resolved to test what they had said.

He made a list – some eighty pages—
Of all the other beverages,
From Absinthe (made in France) to Zlhoo
(Distilled from dates in Timbuctoo),

And tried, with scientific zeal,
A different drink with every meal.

It took the persevering Ned
Four years to work from A to Z,
And when at last he got to 'Finis'
He settled down to try a Guinness.

He poured it out and watched it flow,
Admired its head, its ruby glow,
And thinking 'It looks exquisite'
He tentatively tasted it.

It really was a moving sight
To see his transports of delight
As right into his inmost soul
The goodness of the Guinness stole.
With manly tears his eyes were wet
As rapture mingled with regret
To think of all the years he'd wasted
With this quite peerless drink untasted.

Moral:
No matter where or how you seek,
You'll find that Guinness is unique.

Anonymous

In the years after the Second World War, neon signs were not uncommon in Dublin, but the 'Bovril' advertisment in D'Olier Street became a nine day's wonder, since each of its letters lit up in a different colour. TCD Miscellany *made this comment in June 1951:*

EPITAPH

Here lies one who met his fate
Just outside the College gate;
By darkness saw he sights superb,
With eyes aloft he left the kerb;
As from beneath the 'bus they picked him
They murmured 'Bovril's latest victim.'

Herbert G. FitzGerald

H.G. FitzGerald (c.1896–1920) was at Belvedere College a generation after James Joyce. In 1913 he went on to study law in Trinity College Dublin, where he contributed to TCD Miscellany. *He was always delicate, and not long after he was called to the Bar in 1918, he died.*

His only publication was an affecting book called Rambles, Rhymes and Reminiscences *(1920). Despite a lofty view of popular culture, he found himself sensually drawn to the powdered 'shop-girls' he reproaches, if his verses are to be taken as evidence.*

TWICE NIGHTLY

Snuggling in shilling seats of crimson plush,
Gorging with languid grace on Coffee Creams,
Dublin guffaws, humming the ragtime themes,
At Cockney wit and corybantic slush.

Here shapely, silk-clad female legs demand
Applause from bloodless clerks, with hollow chests;
Here shop-girls snigger at the risky jests
Their embryonic minds just understand.

And in a box, War's stern front retracts
While gallant soldiers smoke with powdered girls,
Whose naked necks and gold (peroxide) curls
Compel all admiration 'twixt the acts.

And over the Proscenium you'll see
The nine sardonic words that did suggest
These lines (writ on a programme leaf) to me—
To hold the mirror up ... you know the rest.

Today, the thought of Dublin in 1916 suggests only one thing. At the time, however, matters were not quite so clear-cut. FitzGerald seems unlikely to have supported the Easter Rising, but he shared with Pearse and the others a sense of dismay that foreign influences were swamping many aspects of Irish life – particularly in the city.

THE GRAFTONETTE, 1916

Will you list, charming maiden of Erin,
To a verse that a worshipper brings?
For your gay life I've taken a share in,
And have noted the following things:
Your complexion most artfully altered,
Your alluring and soft curling lash,
And the way that your glad eyes have faltered
On khaki and cash.

Your hat at an angle erratic
Discloses that you are some girl,
A fact which you make more emphatic
With a tricky, temptation curl.
And lest your fair face will not floor us,
You show us your ankle and calf—
If your style makes your father dolorous,
You girlishly laugh.

For your peek-a-boo's copied from Paris,
And your skirts from your sister of ten,
Your manners, which sometimes embarrass
Your mother, are copied from men.
Your boots seem to flavour of Russia,
Your slang is filched from the States,
Your jostling propensity Prussia,
It seems, instigates.

Your fingers are tastefully yellowed
With the weed that you buy from the Turk,
While our petrol-soaked atmosphere's mellowed
With your perfume that's Persian work.
But your uncontrolled lust after sweets, dear,
And your flapperish passion for cake,
Are assuaged by the Poor in your streets, dear,
Whose sugar you take.

Now here at the end the right place is
To relate, without fear of restraints,
How I view all your soft female graces
In this scholarly City of Saints;
So, raise not your languorous eyelid
With surprise when I say I have seen
A sweet, cosmopolitan hybrid—
Not an Irish Colleen.

Mick Fitzgerald

Mick Fitzgerald (b. 1951) is a man of many talents. He has been – and remains – an actor, a journalist, a writer (most notably of short stories) and a performing musician. From a musical Dublin family, he was a member of the folk group Tipsy Sailor before touring widely in the 1980s with the Wild Geese. Recently, he has issued Light Sleeper, *a CD of his compositions, which he sings with the Bacha Trio. And it is his songwriting skills that concern us here. This irreverent comic ballad has fun with the old divisions between Dublin and the rest of Ireland.*

'Twas at the last election, me brother he went in:
He was always fond of politics, we knew he'd surely win;
He went around, he canvassed hard, he wandered round about,
He said he'd raise the price of milk and bring down the price of stout.

We are the one horse farmers and you know that means damn all—
But now they raise their hats for him, he's a member of the Dáil;
We have a brand new house, you know, we let the old one fall,
For a tigeen wasn't good enough for a member of the Dáil.

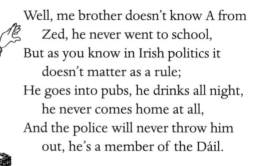

Well, me brother doesn't know A from
    Zed, he never went to school,
But as you know in Irish politics it
    doesn't matter as a rule;
He goes into pubs, he drinks all night,
    he never comes home at all,
And the police will never throw him
    out, he's a member of the Dáil.

On one of his trips to Dublin he
    brought home a brand new wife,
She was the finest bit of stuff I ever saw
    in all me life;
And the three of us sleep together and
    they put me next to the wall—
Still when it's dark she doesn't know
    who's a member of the Dáil.

Me brother's a TD, me boys, me brother's a TD—
He got me Da a pension, he was only forty-three;
Me brother's a TD, me boys, me brother's a TD;
When he's up in Dublin there's plenty of the other for me.

Percy French

Like a human Catherine wheel, Percy French (1854–1920) scattered sparks from his many talents around him wherever he went: stories, paintings, poems, lectures, songs, drawings in candle-smoke on the bottom of dinner-plates, whatever you like. This little-known verse of his was snapped up by A.P. Graves and G. Pertwee for their 1915 anthology, The Reciter's Treasury of Irish Prose and Verse. *It cocks an eyebrow at the reverential treatment generally paid to that now largely extinct breed, the grandee Dublin doctor.*

A CASE OF ETIQUETTE

Sir Diagnosis Stethoscope Parietal De Brown
Was perhaps the most astute of all the medicos in town,
And thro' all his course of study and practice he would let
No sentiment direct him from his code of etiquette.

One evening in the hospital a friend he chanced to see
Being treated for insomnia by Hillary, MD
He saw that Max was treating him most ignorantly, yet
He couldn't interfere – you see it wasn't etiquette.

He vowed the patient couldn't live beneath that upas tree—
'Twas thus that he referred to old Max H., MD
His fingers fairly itched to try his hypodermic jet,
But couldn't well suggest it – as it wasn't etiquette.

The case grew worse – the end drew near, old Max would say, 'Dear me,
There's something I can't fathom here.' De Brown said, 'So I see.'
And when the patient died he went with feelings of regret
And placed a wreath upon his grave
                                    – But this was etiquette.

Anonymous

Though distantly related to 'The German Piano Tuner', set in Manchester, this has been an Irish song for generations. One commentator suggests that it is a rare survival from the 'little known and long discarded Dublin oompah tradition which ticked over until it sent people cuckoo in the nineteenth century'. Grosvenor Square, where the horological consultation takes place, was then a prosperous address in the Rathmines/Harold's Cross area.

THE GERMAN CLOCKWINDER

A German clockwinder to Dublin once came,
Benjamin Fuchs was the old German's name,
And as he was winding his way round the strand,
He played on his flute and the music was grand.

> Chorus:
> Singing …
> Tooralomaloma tooralomaloma tooraliay,

Toorali toorali youraliay,
Tooralomaloma tooralomaloma tooraliay,
Toorali toorali youraliay.

Oh there was a young lady from Grosvenor Square,
Who said that her clock was in need of repair.
In walks the bold German and to her delight,
In less than five minutes he had her clock right.

Now as they were seated down on the floor,
There came this very loud knock on the door.
In walked her husband and great was his shock,
For to see the old German wind up his wife's clock.

Then says the German, 'Sure I meant you no harm,
But the spring wouldn't work in your old wife's alarm.
I pulled out me oil can and I gave it a squirt;
If you keep it well-oiled, your wife's clock will work!'

The husband says he, 'Now look here, Mary Anne,
Don't let that bold German come in here again.
He wound up your clock and left mine
    on the shelf,
If your old clock needs winding, sure I'll
    wind it meself!'

So come all you young fellows, take a
    warning from me,
If the German clockwinder you chance
    for to see,
Take hold of your lassie as firm as a rock,
If you leave her behind, he'll be winding
    her clock.

Leslie Gillespie

Born in Belfast in 1920, Leslie Gillespie published this poem in the 1940–41 winter issue of the New Northman, *a Queen's University student magazine/ literary journal then edited by the poets Robert Greacen and John Gallen. Soon afterwards Gillespie was in wartime India, and he would later write a fine novel there,* The Man from Madura *(1952). He went on to forge close links with Dublin, and contributed variously to* The Bell *and the* Irish Times.

The sardonic lines below take a snapshot of the sort of mildly bohemian party that was common in Dublin even during the 'Emergency': in bomb-ravaged Belfast such organized dissipation was rare enough.

MARCHING THROUGH GEORGIA

J.J. O'Shaughnessy from Rathmines
Sat down at the piano
And as his fingers rippled
Someone struck him with a cigarette-end,
But he didn't indulge in abusive recrimination,
Just glowed with ruminating eyeballs
That were sad, very sad,
Because his heart was telling him
That his trousers were frayed,
His shoes were done,
So he ceased playing 'Marching
   Through Georgia'
And his fingers groped for
   'Nearer my God, to Thee'—
All the while Molly was
   looking,
Slightly amused, puffing at
   a Piccadilly.

Oliver St John Gogarty

George Moore called Oliver Gogarty (1878–1957) 'the author of all jokes that enable us to live in Dublin'. This extremely bawdy set of verses is an affectionate requiem for the 'flash houses' in the Monto area of the city, whose unlicensed after-hours bars had once led young and old alike to indulge in even more illicit pleasures upstairs.

The 'Hay Hotel' in Cavendish Row was where you went after such activities for a cup of coffee and a late-night feed of tripe and onions or crubeens, and so it survived the 1924 purge of Dublin brothels. It was operated by Maria and Stephen, one-time family servants of the Gogartys who had been sacked for being caught on the job. The establishment took its nickname from the fodder piled in a downstairs window to occupy cabbies' horses as they waited for their passengers within.

The sixth stanza below was found on a separate sheet of paper by A.N. Jeffares, editor of The Poems and Plays of Oliver St John Gogarty: *we have inserted it where it seemed to want to go.*

THE HAY HOTEL

There is a window stuffed with hay
Like herbage in an oven cast;
And there we came at break of day
To soothe ourselves with light repast:
And men who worked before the mast
And drunken girls delectable:
A future symbol of our past
You'll, maybe, find the Hay Hotel.

Where are the great Kip Bullies gone,
The Bookies and outrageous Whores
Whom we so gaily rode upon
When youth was mine and youth was yours:

Tyrone Street of the crowded doors
And Faithful Place so infidel?
It matters little who explores
He'll only find the Hay Hotel.

Dick Lynam was a likely lad,
His back was straight; has he gone down?
And for a pal Jem Plant he had
Whose navel was like half a crown.
They were the talk of all Meck town;
And Norah Seymour loved them well;
Of all their haunts of lost renown
There's only left the Hay Hotel.

Fresh Nellie's gone and Mrs Mack,
May Oblong's gone and Number Five,
Where you could get so good a back
And drinks were so superlative;
Of all their nights, O Man Alive!
There is not left an oyster shell
Where greens are gone the greys will thrive;
There's only left the Hay Hotel.

There's nothing left but ruin now
Where once the crazy cabfuls roared;
Where new-come sailors turned the prow
And Love-logged cattle-dealers snored;
The room where old Luke Irwin whored,
The stairs on which John Elwood fell:
Some things are better unencored:
There's only left the Hay Hotel.

Shall Becky Cooper be forgot?
Have I forgotten Liverpool Kate

And all the foam she used to frot
Were she for one night celibate?
I often tried to dam that spate
When 'Fuck me like a horse!' she'd yell,
And who was I to remonstrate
Before I sought the Hay Hotel?

Where is Piano Mary, say,
Who dwelt where Hell's Gates leave the street,
And all the tunes she used to play
Along your spine beneath the sheet?
She was a morsel passing sweet
And warmer than the gates of hell.
Who tunes her now between the feet?
Go ask them at the Hay Hotel.

L'ENVOI
Nay; never ask this week, fair Lord,
If, where they are now, all goes well,
So much depends on bed and board
They give them in the Hay Hotel.

Anonymous

The state of Dublin's waterways has been a matter of concern since records began. By the time this satirical exercise was published (in Pat, *3 December 1881), the dangers of waterborne diseases were well-known, and the City Commissioners had been urgently promising to do something about the problem. Today, the Grand Canal may indeed be cleaner, but it is still not recommended for swimmers (and certainly not for drinkers).*

THE GRAND CANAL

Along the Grand Canal, my boys,
   Which flows through Dublin town,
A man can taste all nature's joys
   In walking up and down.
The gurgling stream flows at his feet,
   Great trees his head o'ershade,
The grassy banks afford a seat
   If he is not afraid.

Afraid! – base thought – what, though he fall,
   The glorious truth is his,
He cannot make the stream at all
   Uncleaner than it is.
Cats, men, and dogs, they crowd the brink,
   Or float this streamlet down,
Which one and all appear to think
   A pleasant place to drown.

For here you see the useful pig
   (I say it with a sigh),
Which doesn't think it *infra dig.*

In Grand Canal to die.
Or perhaps you'll see a noble horse
    Float slowly in towards town,
Which, struck with sorrow, fear, remorse,
    Has rambled in to drown.

But stay – my muse is sad to-night,
    I'll cease the doleful lines,
And tell you of its water bright
    (We drink it in Rathmines);
And who can find us stronger drinks
    In any brewer's vat,
Than this which is composed, methinks,
    Of decomposed Tom-cat!

Commissioners have done full well,
    In fact it was a 'coup,'
To give us water which would sell
    For gravy, meat, or soup.
Then let us boycott Dodder's wave,
    And as each bumper fills
With Grand Canal, we'll swear to save
    Rathmines from butchers' bills.

Bryan Guinness

*The Guinness advertising campaign featuring a menagerie of animals be-
came very celebrated during the middle of the twentieth century. The poet
Bryan Guinness (1905–94) – aka Lord Moyne – proposed a verse to accom-
pany before-and-after illustrations of the benign effects of the family brew,
but his rhyme was never used, possibly because hardly anyone had heard of
this delightful five-toed transatlantic reptile.*

THE AXOLOTL

Behold the slothful axolotl
Drinking from his Guinness bottle;
See him now in finer fettle
Pop up Popocatapetl.

Anonymous

A further helping of social commentary from Pat. *In 1881, the 'land war' led the chief secretary of Ireland, W.E. ('Buckshot') Forster, to press for powers of coercion to balance Gladstone's liberalising reforms. Dublin was 'proclaimed' (i.e. placed under stringent restrictions), and anyone found breaking the terms was arrested. The irony was that innocent travellers from Britain, nervous of attack, felt safer with a firearm. A decade later, on their trip by governess cart through Connemara (still a proclaimed district), even the Irish writers Violet Martin and Edith Somerville thought they needed to pack an illicit, if rusty, revolver in case of 'mad dogs and things on the road'.*

HANDCUFFS FOR TWO WRISTS

Three tourists went sailing out into the west,
    To the Emerald Isle as the fares came down;
Each brought a revolver inside of his vest,
    To protect him from outrage in country and town.
For natives must lurk, and Saxons must keep
An eye on high hedges and ditches deep,
    Their perilous fate bemoaning.

Three 'bobbies' were standing on Kingstown Pier,
  On the Carlisle Pier, as the train came down,
      They searched for revolvers, and found them here;
      (Mr Forster had lately 'proclaimed' the town).
      Police must work, and innocents weep,
      As they're driven in cars to the Dungeon keep,
      Their unlicensed state bemoaning.

Three 'suspects' were lodged in Kilmainham jail;
  Their food was not rich, nor their beds of down;
It were safer to travel in coats of mail
  Than to carry revolvers in Dublin town.
But friends will work, and women will weep,—
If they're out in a year they'll have got off cheap,
  Their holiday trip bemoaning.

Anonymous

Published anonymously in Secret Springs of Dublin Song *(1918), this ballad is set on the edge of the Dublin mountains during the First World War. It is 'reliably rumoured' to have been written by George Redding, civil servant and scurrilous amateur poet, whose centre of operations was for many years the Bailey pub in Duke Street. The action takes place in Lamb Doyle's, one* of many pubs known as 'bona fides' that ringed the outskirts of the city, just far enough from the centre to allow thirsty drinkers to avail of the law that gave genuine (bona fide) travellers the right to an after-hours drink. Naturally, when the city pubs shut each night, there was a general exodus by car to these 'bona fides'.

Could a model for the Hermit have been the bearded theosophist, agriculturalist, painter and poet, Æ (George Russell) – or was it perhaps the Ulster poet Joseph Campbell, whose delight it was to instruct aspiring young druidesses in the arcane arts on the mountain-tops of West Dublin? Any information from readers will be gratefully received by the editors.

THE HERMIT

As I went up by Harold's Grange and down by Sandyford
I thought I saw a sandwich-man without his sandwich-board,
A feather in his Trilby hat; two-buttoned swallow-tail—
A heavy stick was in his hand, a mongrel on his trail.

But as he nearer drew to me I saw that
    there appeared
A fervour in the flashing eyes above the long
    brown beard,
Which held my curiosity the more that I
    thought of it—
Was this dismantled sandwich-man a seer
    or sage or prophet?

A foaming beverage rewards the
    traveller who toils
Along the dusty mountain road that
    leads unto Lamb Doyle's.
I saw which way the hermit went, for ere his mighty stride
Scattered the pebbles in the yard, the door was opened wide.

He passed into that wayside inn unchallenged, unopposed,
While I, who hurried after, heard the door behind him closed,
And found myself confronted with the doorman's questions trite—
'Business or pleasure? Traveller? Where did you sleep last night?'

The seer was seated solemnly before a pint of stout;
He raised a glass as I came in and said to me, 'No doubt
You are a stranger on this road and do not gather quite
The reason why they asked you where it was you slept last night.

'Now listen for a moment while another round they bring
And I will tell you a most ex-traordinary thing;—
This is the Druid's wisdom that the quiet mountains keep—
All health and happiness depend on where a man may sleep.

'Though some men lie on feather beds and some on planks of wood,
I make no difference between the evil and the good;
Last night I lay on Kilmashogue; to-night on Taylor's hill,
I make my bed at eventide, for such it is my will.

'And Power and Glory come to me upon the mountain side
And wizard's secrets known to none since mighty Merlin died;
And all magnetic influence shed on me with the dew,
That I may sway the minds of men, and hearts of women too.'

I may have seemed incredulous – for with suspicious stare
The sage went on: 'As sure as I am sitting in this chair
There is no woman, rich or poor, who will not follow me,
When she has been to my Round House and drunk my laurel tea.

'And though I say these things to you it is not vanity,
Or any virtue in myself but Nature's power in me,
That makes the girls look after me with loving as I pass
Because I drink the magic spring and roll upon the grass.'

The thirsty travellers filled the room
    – it was my time to go,
The Prophet's voice grew louder (he
    saw his audience grow);
I heard his last prediction – 'Now mark
    what my words are—
The night the Kaiser sleeps due west will
    surely end the war.'

Prophet or Hermit, Seer or Sage, throughout my brain
    there ran
Th'experiences of this most ex-traordinary man;
I wondered were they really true, or did I dream them all,
As I went up by Stepaside and down by Golden Ball.

F.R. Higgins

A considerable poet, F.R. Higgins (1896–1941) frustrates literary commentators who like to see a tidy beginning, middle and end to a writer's career. Patrick Kavanagh, looking back at his life in 1946, called him, with some justification, 'The Gallivanting Poet'. Among his enthusiasms was a love of Dublin balladry – in 1935 he even wrote a play, The Deuce of Jacks, *about the blind street-entertainer Zozimus. Today Higgins tends to be overlooked, perhaps because of the variety of tools he used to attack the coalface of verse, but his open character and emotional honesty shine through his best writing.*

THE OLD JOCKEY

His last days linger in that low attic
That barely lets out the night,

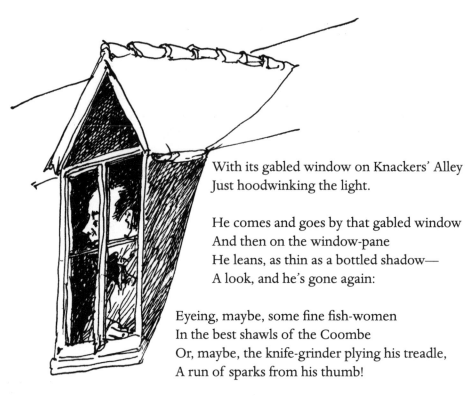

With its gabled window on Knackers' Alley
Just hoodwinking the light.

He comes and goes by that gabled window
And then on the window-pane
He leans, as thin as a bottled shadow—
A look, and he's gone again:

Eyeing, maybe, some fine fish-women
In the best shawls of the Coombe
Or, maybe, the knife-grinder plying his treadle,
A run of sparks from his thumb!

But O you should see him gazing, gazing
When solemnly out on the road
The horse drays pass overladen with grasses,
Each driver lost in his load;

Gazing until they return; and suddenly,
As galloping by they race,
From his pale eyes, like glass breaking,
Light leaps on his face.

T.C. Irwin

Though Donnybrook Fair had been going since King John instituted it in 1205,
by Victorian times it was so famous for attracting drunks and brawlers that
the phrase 'a fair day's donnybrook' had come to mean an affray. One defend-
ant in a manslaughter trial protested that if the skull of his victim was as
thin as the coroner said, he shouldn't have been at a fair in the first place.

In fact, by day, it was perfectly safe, and every year many thousands of
Dubliners flocked to the fields between Stillorgan and Donnybrook to see fit-
up theatres, acrobats and other amusements, and to dine for a penny by fish-
ing for lumps of bacon boiling in a pot. The British Army purchased many
of its cavalry horses there. By night, however, the Fair justified its violent
reputation, and so in 1857 the Corporation heeded calls for the 'abatement of
this deleterious nuisance', and had it discontinued.

Thomas Caulfield Irwin (1823–92) was an accomplished poet, whose
sonnets on nature are still interesting, though they are not now much read.
His elegy for the passing of the Fair is uncharacteristically jolly and 'stage-
Irish', but the tone well suits the subject. The poem bears the subtitle 'A Lay
of the Last Minstrel of the Liberty'.

A LAMENT FOR DONNYBROOK

Jimmy, aghar, hand me my pipe,
   In truth I'm as wearied as man can be;
   My eye is as dim as the winter sea,
And my nose as sharp as the bill of a snipe;
For here for a week, a week and more,
I have been labouring body and sowl,
   Just sustained by whiskey and sassages,
   While I touch the finishing passages
Of my Donnybrook rigmarole.

Saints be about us! what are they driving at?
  All sorts of people are taking their share—
All have their heads together conniving at—
  At the destruction of Donnybrook Fair.
Once in the good ould times of the city,
  MPs, farmers, the rich, and the rare,
Gentlemen, nobles, the wise and the witty,
  Went for a trifle of element there.
Then was the rale indulgement in jollity,—
  Devil a one of them cared who was who!
  All took their glass of the mountain dew,
And their hop in the tent on the ground of equality.
But now it is over, – this is the last of them—
  This is the last ould fair that we'll see;
Now we must live as we can on the best of them—
  Such is the Corporation's decree.

Ah, never again in this isle shall be seen
    The rale boys up to the sweet oaken science!
    Trailing their coats in courageous defiance,
And shouting the pillalu over the green.
Never again shall we see the shillelagh
    Joyously splintering forehead and limb,
Or hear Molly Finucane crying, 'Oh, mela
    Murder! what have you done with my Jim?'
Never again 'mid the turmoil or rattle
    Shall we assemble to shoulder the door,
Bearing dear friends, through the thick of the battle,
    Faithfully home to their widows, asthore:—

Leaving the pleasant old ground, when the short night
    Of August was melting in matinal dew,
    With a rib or two dinged or an eye black and blue,
Or a wound that would lay us up snug for a fortnight:
While a rattle of sticks in the distance behind
Made old Donnybrook look like a wood in a wind.
    Now all is over, – this is the last of them,—
        This is the last ould fair that we'll see;
    Now we must live as we can on the past of them—
        Such is the Corporation's decree.

Anonymous

In 1920 W.H. McLaughlin exhumed these lines for an anthology, presumably from some newspaper or magazine of the 1860s. They give a whiff of the tensions in what we now call 'colonial' Ireland – mentioning, for example, the wrangles that had been going on between the Cork-born MP John Pope Hennessy and the Chief Secretary for Ireland Sir Robert Peel.

McLaughlin added a note above the verses to the effect that they were written after the government decreed that no 'party tunes' should be played in the Irish section of the 1862 Great Exhibition of the Works of Industry of All Nations, held in South Kensington. Several tunes are named, but none is in any way seditious – and the odd one out is 'Garryowen', a stirring melody that had led many British soldiers into battle, and had been adopted as the Regimental March of the Royal Irish Regiment.

IT WAS AT DARLING DUBLIN

The songs of Erin are always charmin',
Though sometimes alarmin'
   In their fiery mood;
He's a real rapscallion,
Who says Italian
   Or German music is half so good.

It was at darlin' Dublin,
At the Exhibition,
They had no suspicion – of 'Garryowen';

Though Mozart and Handel
Can't hould a candle
　　To the 'Groves of Blarney' or 'Widow Malone.'
Out spoke Pope Hennessy,
With a voice of menace, he
　　Defended Erin and astounded Peel;
Alas and well-a-day,
Of native melody,
　　Barbarian noises do now prevail.
But when German dreaming
And Italian screaming
　　Entirely vanished and forgotten are;
Then Erin's daughter
Will sing 'Boyne Water,'
　　As she drives to market on her low-backed car.

Anonymous

'De Night before Larry was Stretch'd' is the best-known of a group of darkly comic songs that were written towards the end of the eighteenth century in a sort of Dublin cant – sometimes inaccurately called a 'thieves argot'. 'Jemmy O'Brien's Minuet' is another of them: it appeared in print in Paddy's Resource (1802).

　　In contrast to the other songs in the sequence, there is no sympathy for the condemned man here. Jemmy O'Brien was a Dublin Castle employee; as the folklorist and historian Terry Moylan explains, he worked for 'Town Major (i.e. Police Chief) Charles Henry Sirr at the time of the United Irishmen. His duties included those of the "stag" (informer), enforcer, hitman and perjurer. He is said to have sent many men to the gallows by either falsely swearing away their lives from the witness box, or by personally taking their lives himself.'

The on-stage delivery of the song about this classic Irish turncoat must have been a mini-opera in itself. Between verses Jemmy bemoans his fate in demotic prose, until halfway through the song there is a change of register, and the language becomes mock-heroic. Then Dublinese returns again for the actual 'performance' and as Jemmy is silenced, the commentary is taken over by an ebullient master of ceremonies.

Though a note under the title of the song says that it was performed at 'De Sheriff's Ridotto, No. 1, Green Street', this was no place of entertainment, despite the name. Green Street was the location of both the new Court House and the Newgate Prison, the joke being that Jemmy's 'minuet' (or 'minit') was danced on the gallows.

JEMMY O'BRIEN'S MINUET

Tune: De night before Larry was stretch'd.

Oh! De night before Jemmy was stretch'd,
De spies de all ped him a visit,
And swore, now de Coleman was ketch'd,
'Twas in vain any longer to quiz it;
His crimes and his murders found out,
Convicted and cast was de Bully,
And de lad dat so many did out,
Must at last be tuck'd up to de pulley,
    Bekays he was doom'd to de Gad.

> Ah Major jewel! is dere no hopes a-tall a-tall? Sure Corny wouldn't be so hard hearted as for to come for to go for to dizzart a suffering loyalist in trouble! G–d's bleak boys, why didn't the judge recommend de jury to find him noncum piss mentus? – But what signifies sniv'ling – de game is up, and its what we must all come to.
>   Li, toll de roll, &c.

Poor Jemmy den hung down his head,
And his spirits began for to falter;
His knees knockt together with dread
Of to-morrow's damn'd squeeze from de halter;
Said he, 'Brother bravoes and spies,
Take warning from my sishuation;
Now justice for vengeance loud cries,
So you can't long escape condemnation.'
    For vengeance at last will come down.

      Ah, boys never depend upon de castle! Be de hokey I swore as
much on de Holy Evangelists in de sweet cause of loyalty as
would blister a griddle, and 'till dere was a crust upon my soul
a fut tick, and now you see, I'm to be snitch'd for a lousy mur-
der. But never mind dat. Who'd regard a bit of an oat upon an
ould greasy bible, or want a genteel income in blood-money,
for de sake of a few scruples about murder and perjury, and de
like o' dat?
      Li, toll de roll, &c.

'Oh,' den said de spies, one and all;
Reflecting on poor Jemmy's sentence,
'Our crimes are too deep to recall,
And quite too far gone for repentance.
Av tyranny we've been de tools,
What murders we've caused thro' de nation,
Yet lucky we'll be – if such fools
De gallice can save from damnation;'
    And so de bid Jemmy good night.

61

Tune: Welcome, welcome brother debtor.

All gloomy dawned the fatal morning,
When to Jemmy's dungeon door,
The hangman came, with woeful warning,
And found him writhing on the floor.
The scorpion stings of conscience wounding
His guilty heart with countless crimes,
When rous'd, he heard his death-knell sounding
In the clink of Newgate chimes.

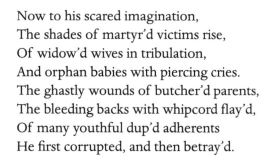

Now to his scared imagination,
The shades of martyr'd victims rise,
Of widow'd wives in tribulation,
And orphan babies with piercing cries.
The ghastly wounds of butcher'd parents,
The bleeding backs with whipcord flay'd,
Of many youthful dup'd adherents
He first corrupted, and then betray'd.

His cell with fancy'd shrieks resounded,
Of those his perjuries destroy'd.
Despair his hell-fraught mind confounded,
Whilst horror ev'ry nerve annoy'd.
Mean time, Tom, around his throttle,
Gently fix'd the fatal nooze
He bid him take a chearful bottle,
For he had now no time to lose.

Mr. O'Brien, jewel! make haste wid your prayers and long life to
you! For your wantin widout, de sideboard is up, and de sheriff
says he can't stay – moreover, de congregation is all waiting for
you under de swing swong.
    Li, toll de roll, &c.

So Jemmy plucked up a stout heart,
Wid de last puff of spunk dat was in it,
Prepar'd for to sport all his art
In moving de Kilmainham minit.
De corps of informers and spies
Came to take de last leave o' deir chroney,
And heartily blasted his eyes
    Dat his deat left his chums no blood-money.

Major, jewel! keep up your spirits, for grief is all fudge. Never
lament for poor Jemmy, as he's only gone a step before you.
Gallice Paul's luck to his friend 'Ould Towler' dat didn't put in
a point to save his neck, and send him to sweet Botany instead
of de squeezer.
    Li, toll de roll, &c.

Tom tould him – he must walk up stairs,
Den Jem turn'd out of de grotto,
Dough bashful, to dance he prepares
A new jigg at de Sheriff's ridotto.
But when he came to de swing swong,
De buffer was seized wid de vapours,
To tink dat he lasted so long,
    For a hearty-choak brekfast and capers.

Den de gallice mob took off deir beavers and gave dir ould
friend three cheers and a screech. Hurrah, success Jemmy
darlint! Welcome home at last – Is Ivers from Carlow come?
– Where's T. Reynolds, dat you haven't him to play for your
benefit? – Ah, be de hokey, dere's two a wantin; but all in good
time – Now your souls! Honour de new performer – Dis is Mr.

O'Brien's first appearance upon de Sheriff's stage – let us give him a good clap and three cheers upon de first kick.

Li, toll de roll, &c.

So Jemmy now fixt in de frame,
For de well disarv'd end of his labours,
Dough scragg'd in confusion and shame,
It was all by consent of his neighbours.
He gracefully pulled down his cap,
And turned his mug tow'rds de Liffey,
Den down fell de leaf wid a flap,
    And he dy'd, wid three kicks, in a jiffey.

Hirrau, boys – success to de necklace trade, and de same luck to de rest o' de family. Be de hokey, whenever de come here dey'll have a full benefit, barring de snigg der own wizzards and bilk de hangman … but Hell will never be full till de come and de devil receives dem all in his holy clutches.

Paul Jones

Lord Nelson was always an uneasy guest on the pillar that dominated Dublin's main street until 1966, when, as predicted, the IRA blew him off as a statement of Irish liberation. But though songs galore were written to celebrate that glorious event, in reality most people missed the 'old one-handled adulterer', as Joyce called him in Ulysses.

The following appeal for clemency appeared in Dublin Opinion *long before the explosion. Like most of that grossly underestimated magazine (which was founded in 1922 and continued until the 1960s), the poem was written by the cartoonist, water-colourist and writer Charles E. Kelly and his long-term co-editor, Tom Collins, who shared the characteristically unassuming pseudonym.*

A PLEA FOR NELSON PILLAR

Dauntless aloft he sails the skies
    An admiral of stone,
Watching with, doubtless, quiet eyes
    A country not his own
Whose memories of sailormen are Bantry Bay and Tone.

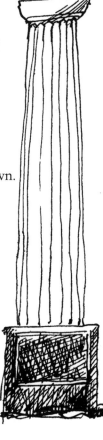

Only when winds are from the South
    He sees Trafalgar Bay
And hears the belching cannon-mouth
    Wreak wreck and disarray,
Giving, with empty sleeve close-hauled, the order of
    the day.

Long buried is that battle's bane,
    Still stands the column's stone.
We took the Norman and the Dane
    And made of them our own;
And the tall shaft of alien birth to one of us has grown.

I'm sure 'twas scarcely up a year,
    As Davis would have said,
When it became a 'Dubliner'
    To Dubliners long dead.
The way the Geraldines once trod was plainly its
    to tread.

Our winds around its granite pate
    A hundred years have blown,
I think if we could put it straight
    To Theobald Wolfe Tone,
His vote would be: 'Don't spoil the street.
    Let the old chap alone.'

Charlie Keegan

Charlie Keegan has been writing verse for years, although he earns his living in the world of traditional music – which he calls 'poetry without words'. These perfectly formed lines were inspired by a close encounter in his mother's garden.

ODE TO A GIANT SNAIL FOUND
IN A DUBLIN GARDEN

You might think you're great
O mighty mollusc,
But my garden plants think you're
An almighty bollusc.

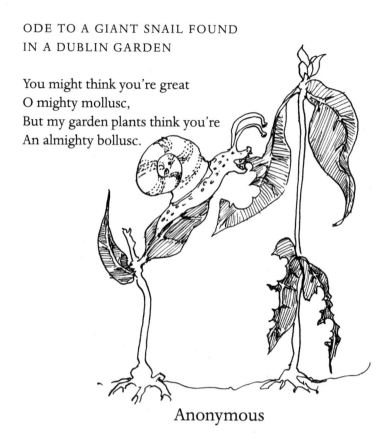

Anonymous

It has been impossible to resist this nicely observed vignette, found in Pat, *7 May 1881, largely because it exactly echoes a recent experience of the writer of these notes.*

I met a friend in Grafton-street,
   Who stopped me on my way,
His air was grand, his dress was neat,
   His spirits light and gay.

He asked me how I was, and when
   I had arrived in town;
He asked for all the news, and then—
   He asked for half-a-crown.

Francis Ledwidge

Francis Ledwidge (1891–1917) is sometimes thought of as an Irish Edward Thomas or Rupert Brooke, because he was killed at Ypres. In fact, he had more in common with writers like John Clare, or perhaps in Ireland Padraic Colum.

In this parody of the stirring 'The Burial of Sir John Moore' (by another Leinster man, Charles Wolfe), the Romantic Celt gives way to the entertainer. Ledwidge volunteered for the 5th Royal Inniskilling Fusiliers in 1914, reckoning that the British Army was Ireland's only line of defence against the Germans. 'Billy the Bulldog' first saw the light a year later in Inchicore, Dublin, in the recreation rooms of Richmond Barracks, where the poet sometimes amused his comrades by reading them his 'occasional' verses.

Billy was the Regimental mascot. He had a personality that, as so often among those who choose a military career, became increasingly difficult and dangerous as he grew older. Liam O'Meara (editor of the 1997 Complete Poems) explains, 'Rather than have him put down he was given to a lady of one of the officers who looked after him until he died. So loved was he, that a headstone, fully inscribed, was erected to him.' That was no doubt the case, but Ledwidge's elegy reveals that the men may not have mourned Billy for too long.

THE DEPARTURE OF BILLY THE BULLDOG

Not a bark was heard nor a sigh nor moan
When they put the chain around him,
But quiet he munched a cow's thigh-bone
By the side of the man who found him.
He broke the rules and he had to go,
Let he who may lament him,
The Army orders would have it so
And silently we sent him.
Say, have we loved his twisted face?
Have we loved his sly cold manner?
Say, is there soldier in the place
Would sell him twice for a tanner?
Ask at the cook-house door today
Will they miss his noonday calls there?
Ask of the Transport, what do they say?
There! Nought but sighs and brawls there.
He bit the horses and chased the mules,
So they gave him a court martial
And despite the strictness of the rules
Was the jurisdiction partial.
His transfer papers we made out
Tho' it's many the tear that wet them
And he went away to the feeble shout
Of the few who won't forget him.

William Russell MacDonald

The rotund pomposity of Alderman Sir William Curtis, twice Lord Mayor of London, made him the constant butt of idle satirists. 'Sir Billy Biscuit', as they called him – his father had baked them for ships – was said to be illiterate. He apparently once insisted that King Henry III had lived before King Henry II, and was credited with quite innocently coining the phrase, 'The Three Rs', in a serious speech about education.

Masquerading as one of Tom Moore's latest 'Melodies', these abusive verses about him appeared in 1821 in a scurrilous volume of spoof letters between Dublin and London, The Dublin Mail, *or Intercepted Correspondence, by William Russell MacDonald (1784–1854). Evidently the Alderman's recent visit to Dublin had been punctuated by much fine dining at the table of Mr Morrison, 'the prince of cooks in Dublin'. There was also a ludicrous episode when he was mistaken for his friend King George IV and was chaired around the city by an excited crowd, until it was realized that His Majesty had a rather daintier nose.*

A NEW IRISH MELODY

There's an Alderman here looking foolish and fat,
    With cheeks not much given to dimples;
With a mouth full as wide as a large brewer's vat,
    And a nose richly studded with pimples.

He waddles along with abundance of Grace,
    Though sometimes cast down from deep thinking;
And few could mistake from one look at his face
    That he's dreaming of eating and drinking!

He has written a volume on every dish—
    'Tis a learned and eloquent treatise;

On turtle, and ven'son, and wild-fowl, and fish,
    Which he gave Mr. MORRISON gratis!

His exquisite taste ages yet will admire,
    When the Alderman down in the earth is;
And cooks of both sexes get drunk o'er the fire,
    In pledging thy fame, BILLY C——s!

M.J. MacManus

M.J. MacManus (1888–1951) was born in Carrick-on-Shannon, Co. Leitrim, but spent his younger years in England and much of the rest of his life in Dublin. He was popular for his comic prose and verse, though the first poem here from our selection of three can scarcely be called funny. It comes from a 1928 collection called Dublin Diversions. *Given his evident anger about the evasions and agonies that had ushered in the new Ireland, it is interesting to learn that three years later MacManus would agree to act as literary editor on Eamon de Valera's* Irish Press.

REMEMBRANCE

I fear there was something very wrong
With that little war of ours,
Or we would laud its deeds with song
And pretty flags and flowers.
It wasn't, I think, a respectable war,
A really proper, civilised war,
It was, in fact, an amateur war,
That little war of ours.

We had no uniforms at all
(A thing that isn't done),
And we never hearkened to the call
To go and fight the Hun.
But we fought at home a raggedy war,
A most unpleasant, unmannerly war,
In fact, a most un-English war,
That little war we won.

We honour Dublin's Fusiliers
(Right gallantly they fell
When the cry went up for volunteers
To storm the gates of hell).
But that was a really glorious war,
A rescue-poor-little-Belgium war,
An altogether different war
From the war in Dublin town,

If ever we shoulder guns again
When the gage of war is thrown,
We'll find a nation smaller far
(If possible) than our own.
And when it's attacked we'll wage a war,
A world-safe-for-democracy war,
A high, religious, heavenly war,
A war unlike our own.

And then the flowers will blossom red
In the streets of Dublin town,
And our lame and crippled and blind and dead
Will be men of high renown.
But it must be a really respectable war,
An orderly, capitalistic war,
A God-damned, hypocritical war,
To be honoured in Dublin town.

IN
GLORIOUS
MEMORY
of the fallen,
In Ireland's support
of the liberation of
Oiléan na Fír
(former Isle of Man)

MacManus's 1939 volume, A Green Jackdaw, *is subtitled 'Adventures in Parody'. 'Eden Quay' is an entirely convincing appropriation of the delicate style of James Stephens's verse; it also wittily demonstrates his famous remark: 'Dublin is less an aggregation of buildings than a collection of personages.'*

EDEN QUAY

The jarvey shivered in the rain,
Blew upon his fingers, and
Muttered things that were profane,
Wishing somebody would stand
A pint or two, a pint or two;
And so would you, and so would you.

Another Green Jackdaw *spoof, which visits the not-so-distant glory days when Dublin seemed thronged with literary and political giants. This was the city that Susan Mitchell used to send up in her comic verse – and curiously, she too came from Carrick-on-Shannon. MacManus uses her teasing poems about the novelist George Moore as reference points – the originals may be found in* Ireland's Other Poetry.

A LAMENT FOR THE DAYS THAT ARE GONE

There was a day, a far-off day, a day we'll see no more,
When in our witty city there were playboys by the score,
And my coruscating *jeux d'esprit* kept Dublin in a roar.

They're staid and sober now who then were sowing their wild oats,
Who wore the broad and flowing tie and sported velvet coats,
And thought it was a daring thing to shout for women's votes.

Sinn Féin was then an idle phrase on idle breezes blown,
And the British Commons nightly heard the Party monotone,
While Dublin wits from paper slings threw many a jagged stone.

Æ was not so weighty then, a fire was in his eyes,
Poor Synge was making Abbey Street resound with faction cries,
And WB had never dreamt of any Nobel Prize.

Those were the days when wickedly I fashioned rhymes sardonic
To help George Moore when he complained of troubles gastronomic,
And found for him (and others, too) a never-failing tonic.

My classic joke is still recalled of Moore's divine grey mullet,
The only fish that would not stick in his fastidious gullet;
But now he shakes a leg elsewhere – and so I cannot pull it.

His books are now respectable – we
thought them naughty then—
For stars with far more lurid flames
have sailed into our ken,
And even George would jib at things
from Mister Joyce's pen.

The playboys are all gone from us,
the years are closing in,
The jokes (though not their subjects)
are growing somewhat thin;
The comic days are over – let the sad
years now begin!

Anonymous

Once we had encountered this unforgettable 'monologue in song' about an unlikely crime, we couldn't leave it out. It was once recorded by that great Dublin songster, the late Frank Harte. If anyone can date it, or better still, tell us who wrote it, the editors would be most grateful.

THE MAID OF CABRA WEST

I'll tell you a tale of a fair young maid
That in Cabra West did reside.
Meself, I live up in Donnybrook—
It's a one-and-a-fipenny ride;
But there was a fly in the ointment now
That you very seldom see,
For although I loved her terrible well—
She was in love with a Portugee.

Now he was a nasty piece of goods,
Gonzales was his name,
And he couldn't wait till he got his hands
On Concepta – who was me dame;
So I made a vow be the Grand Canal
That I would do him in,
'Cos I didn't think much of them Portugees
And in particular – I didn't like him.

So I follied them up to Grafton Street
One evenin' just for fun,
Around by the Mercer's Hospital
Next door to the Bartley Dunne;
Sure I spied them sittin' in the corner seat,

They was kissin' and holdin' hands.
Ah! There he was seducing her—
With pints of Babycham.

So I follied him up to his lodgings
In Rathgar or thereabouts,
And as he was going up an alleyway
I battered him inside out;
He gave out many's the curse and swear
Till he was dead, I'm sure—
Then I lifted up a manhole lid
And dropped him down the sewer.

Now when the mot she heard of this
Sure she made me life a hell,
So just for the sake of peace and quiet
I did her in as well;
And it's now I'm up before the judge
To answer for me crime—
He says, 'I wouldn't mind the first one, son,
Ah, but not the second time.'

So it's all for the love of that fair young maid
And her Portugee sailor boy,
For the passionate love of that fair young maid
I landed in Mountjoy;
And if ever I get out again
I'll change me ways, you'll see
And I'll marry with a woman from Walkinstown
Who wouldn't look at a Portugee!

M.J.F. Mathews and Fergus Allen

My love's an arbutus
By the borders of Lene,
So slender and shapely
In her girdle of green;
And I measure the pleasure
Of her eye's sapphire sheen,
By the blue skies that sparkle
Thro' that soft branching screen.

The lines above are from the beginning of a once famous poem by Alfred Per-
cival Graves, in which the poet's beloved is likened to one of Killarney's cel-
ebrated 'Strawberry Trees' (Arbutus Unedo). Graves's ridiculous effusion
has now returned to the obscurity it deserves. To help it on its way, Michael
Mathews (c.1922–65) produced the following parody for TCD Miscellany in
the mid-1940s.

A POEM
(With sincere apologies to Alfred Percival Graves)

My love is an incubus,
God only knows,
From her exquisite head
To her elegant toes.

My love is an incubus
Such the hard truth,
Though she's long in the lashes
And short in the tooth.

My love is an incubus,
So let it be;

I love my love dearly;
She tolerates me.

My love is an incubus,
Perish all doubt,
My loves asks champagne,
When I can't afford stout.

That was not the end of the story. Soon afterwards, a parody of that parody also appeared in TCD. *It was written by a friend of Michael Mathews, Fergus Allen (more of whose work can be found at the beginning of this book).*

THIS MAN'S MEAT
(With apologies to M.J.F. Mathews)

My love is an omnibus
Carry 'em all,
Like expandible trunks
And the stand in the hall.

My love is an omnibus,
Smoking on top,
You should hold up your hand
If you want her to stop.

My love is an omnibus,
No dogs inside,
When there isn't a crowd
I can go for a ride.

My love is an omnibus,
Stand near the front,

The springs of her chassis
Are bearing the brunt.

My love is an omnibus,
Have your fare ready,
Internal combustion's
A trifle unsteady.

Ewart Milne

Ewart Milne (1903–87) spent most of his life outside Ireland. The following ballad reveals a certain sensitivity about his reputation at home. It comes from a section called 'Parodies and Pixillated Pieces' in our favourite Milne collection, Once More to Tourney *(1958). The identity of the tall poet in the second verse is easily solved – 'Kerr's Ass' was a poem written by Patrick Kavanagh. Precisely what the 'Ging Gong Goo' might be must remain for the reader to decide.*

THE BALLAD OF GING GONG GOO

As I was going up Grafton Street
A pretty young girl I thought there I would meet,
I said to her: Sweetling how do you Do?
But she answered pertly: With your Ging Gong Goo!

As I was walking by Harold's Cross
A poet I met riding Kerr's big jackass,
Said Lofty: There's sorra the one will remember YOU.
But I answered and said: How's your Ging Gong Goo!

As I was strolling through Stephen's Green
A gaggle of critics came on the scene,
Said they: A modicum of merit's our
  rating for YOU.
The same, said I, for your Ging Gong Goo!

I saluted Nelson as I passed him by,
I raised my hat to his stoneblind eye,
I said to Nelson: Our hearts are true!
But a blind eye answered: So's my
  Ging Gong Goo!

    * * * *

Many blessings light on the Ging Gong Goo,
May it be cursed to Hell and back again, too,
May the Ging Gong Goo forever fail
May it bitch the dog and wag the tail.
I'll never part with my Ging Gong Goo.
Do you like it? Ging Gong Goo.

Anonymous

The Molly Malone we all know, endlessly wheeling her barrow of bivalves through Dublin's thoroughfares, is surely predated by this one, a girl of great charm who bears a greater resemblance to a young Molly Bloom than to the famous fishmonger. From The Irish Comic Song Book, *a compilation dating from around 1860 that contains several ephemeral early nineteenth-century ballads and ditties.*

MOLLY MALONE

By the big hill of Howth,
    That's a bit of an oath,
That to swear by it I'm loth,
    To the heart of a stone,
But be poison my drink,
    If I sleep, snore, or wink,
Once, forgetting to think
    Of your lying alone,
        Sweet Molly, sweet Molly Malone.
        Sweet Molly, sweet Molly Malone.

Och! It's now I'm in love,
    Like a beautiful dove,
That sits cooing above,
    In the boughs of a tree!
It's myself I'll soon smother,
    In something or other,
Unless I can bother
    Your heart to love me.
        Sweet Molly, sweet Molly Malone.
        Sweet Molly, sweet Molly Malone.

I can see if you smile,
　　Though I'm off half a mile,
For my eyes all the while
　　Keep along with my head;
And my head, you must know,
　　When from Molly I go,
Takes his leave with a bow,
　　And remains in my stead.
　　　　Sweet Molly, sweet Molly Malone.
　　　　Sweet Molly, sweet Molly Malone.

Like a bird I could sing,
　　In the month of the spring,
But it's no such a thing,
　　I'm quite bothered and dead.
Och! I'll roar and I'll groan,
　　My sweet Molly Malone,
'Till I'm bone of your bone,
　　And asleep in your bed.
　　　　Sweet Molly, sweet Molly Malone.
　　　　Sweet Molly, sweet Molly Malone.

Anonymous

Another curiosity that appears in The Irish Comic Song Book. *The version there lacks verses 2 and 5, which we have added from an extraordinary travesty of a book published in 1821 by Pierce Egan (1772–1849), entitled* Real Life in Ireland, or, the Day and Night Scenes, Rovings, Rambles, and Sprees, Bulls, Blunders, Bodderation and Blarney of Brian Boru, Esq., and his Elegant Friend Sir Shawn O'Dogherty; Exhibiting a Real Picture of Characters, Manners, etc., in High and Low Life in Dublin ... by a Real Paddy. *Though to today's tastes the whole thing may reek of stage-Irishry, the portrait of the optimistic old alcoholic soldier is not without sympathy.*

MURROUGH O'MONAGHAN

At the side of the road, near the bridge of Drumcondra,
    Was Murrough O'Monaghan stationed to beg;
He had brought from the war, as his share of the plunder,
    A crack on the crown and the loss of a leg.
'Oagh, Murrough!' he'd cry, 'musha nothing may harm you,
    What made you go fight for a soldier on sea?
You fool, had you been a marine in the army,
    You'd now have a penshion and live on full pay.'

'I've an eye,' he would say, 'on the field of Vittoria,
    Looking out for the foe, if they come back to Spain;
My leg is at Waterloo rotting in glory,
    'Twill never conduct me to glory again;
A piece of my sconce was at Leipsic blown up,
    And went off with the bridge in a terrible roar,
I was fairly knock'd but not fairly knock'd up,
    For still I exist to drink whiskey galore.'

'But now I'm a cripple, what argufies thinking?
    The past I can never bring round to the fore:
The heart that with old age and weakness is sinking,
    Will ever find strength in good whiskey galore!
Oagh, whiskey, mavourneen, my joy and my jewel!
    What signifies talking of doctors and pills?
In sorrow, misfortune, and sickness so cruel,
    A glass of North-Country can cure all our ills.'

'When cold, in the winter, it warms you so hearty;
    When hot, in the summer, it cools you like ice;
In trouble – false friends, without grief I can part you,
    Good whiskey's my friend, and I take its advice!
When hungry and thirsty 'tis meat and drink to me;
    It finds me a lodging wherever I lie;
Neither frost, snow, nor rain, any harm can do me,—
    The hedge is my pillow, my blanket the sky.'

'O Ireland! dear country! congenial for begging,
    How gladly I look on thy green hills again;

My dear native mud I at ease stick my peg in,
    Nor painfully stump it through Gallia and Spain;
With a can of sweet butter-milk fresh in the morning,
    And at dinner sweet murphys boil'd up by the score,
I live like a fighting cock, dunghill birds scorning,
    And at supper I revel in whiskey galore.'

'Now, merry be Christmas! success to good neighbours,
    Here's a happy new year, and a great many too!
With plenty of whiskey to lighten their labours,
    May sweet luck attend every heart that is true!'
Poor Murrough then joining his two hands together,
    High held up the glass, while he vented this prayer,—
'May whiskey, by sea or by land, and all weathers,
    Be never denied to the children of care!'

Anonymous

Trinity College has always been an island of calm in the busy centre of Dublin and, as far back as the 1930s, when the lines below were written, the frenetic bustle of the city could be almost too much for undergraduates who dared to venture outside the gates. Under the initials 'EMG', these verses appeared on 10 February 1938 in TCD Miscellany *– or, as it sometimes called itself in those days, 'Miss Ella Knee'.*

O'CONNELL BRIDGE

The Garda lifts his snow-white hand,
The traffic dragon grunts and stops;
Two fertile matrons cross the street,
Four eyes regard the fashion shops.

The newsboy flings a glance against
The vacant eyes of passers-by,
Advertisements cry: 'Gas, use Gas,'
The matrons see the price and sigh.

The Garda flicks his chaste white hand,
The dragon growls, moves on again;
A blood-red sign above me cries:
'What of that sharp abdominal pain?
What of those spots before your eyes?'

Charles O'Flaherty

In the eighteenth and nineteenth centuries, many witty verses were written for Dublin's various 'Convivial Societies' (or drinking clubs). In winter members met in city hostelries, while in summer bulging hampers were brought to Howth or Glendalough, where they would sit on rugs reciting their compositions to each other.

The journalist Charles O'Flaherty was a stalwart of 'The Hermits', and for one of their 'Hebdominal Meetings' he composed the following song. It was written in about 1816, after the famous balloonists, Sadler and Livingston, had ascended from Richmond Barracks, and then 'descended at Night in the Bog of Allen, and were rescued by a Dog'.

According to the Freeman's Journal, *the rescue by the dog actually happened: the night was so dark that the intrepid pair might have drowned in a boghole if a barking dog hadn't led them to a farmhouse. They were so grateful that they adopted the 'Jowler' on the spot.*

With nonsense words added as a chorus, it can be sung to the air of 'The Irish Phantasmagoria' (which we have failed to trace).

THE AERONAUTS

Oh! did you not hear of the famous Balloon,
How SADLER shook hands with the Man in the Moon,
The Mob was so eager, the sight to behold,
Such Noddies, and Jingles, and Carriages roll'd,
And myself run so fast, faith I caught a big cold.

The day was so hazy, 'twould hardly go up,
So to keep out the cold, faith myself took a sup,
And so the two heroes were lost in the fog,
They reckon'd no mile stones – but fell in a bog,
And both were ask'd home by a true Irish Dog.

'Twas Night when they follow'd their four-footed guide,
The door of his Cabin stood smiling so wide,
That each whisper'd th' other, 'We now have the odds,
This visit is better than that to the Gods;'
So the Dog stirr'd the fire, and put down a few sods.

When the blazing turf warm'd the wanderers legs,
The Dog did the honours – but *they* did the eggs,
But first they drank, out of the real Inishone,
The health of the Dog, and they then drank their own,
And bless'd their kind Host, who such favour had shewn.

In the morning then, after their rural shake down,
To the Village they walk'd, for a Carriage to Town,
And says SADLER, 'We surely may now travel post,
For there's you and there's I, and the third is our Host,
And sure among three 'tis a trifle at most.'

In a Post-Chaise and Four, then they gallop'd away,
And wherever they came sure the mob did 'Huzza',
For Jowler was placed, and two heroes between,
And the ship-wreck'd Balloon, on the roof it was seen,
And they made no delay until in College-green.

Liam O'Meara

Liam O'Meara (b. 1953) is a Dublin writer and historian. An expert on Francis Ledwidge (also to be found in these pages), he is currently working on a history of Richmond Barracks. As a poet, he has a verse autobiography to his name, and has won many prizes for his work. None of them can have been as rewarding, however, than hearing that the great Limerick poet, the late Michael Hartnett, loved the poem below.

MOVING STATUES

Not the Virgin Mary
but the halo of Saint Joseph
moved from its spot
in the church at Ballyfermot.
It was after the priest

told the congregation
that the halo was made of gold.
That night it moved,
flitted about the moonlit church
and it was seen no more.

Anonymous

This barefaced example of paddywhackery was published in Victorian times by the Glasgow firm of John S. Marr in The Dublin Songster, *an (undated) collection of ballads and lyrics. It was apparently designed to be sung to the air, 'The Priest in his Boots', and it would be interesting to hear*

this attempted, if only to solve the mystery of how it might be put across to
an audience. As it stands, the bizarre chorus is almost impossible to read
out loud.

Of the more obscure words in the song, a 'spalpeen' here simply means
a ruffian – from the word for a casual farm labourer – but we have been de-
feated by 'taef' in the second verse.

PADDY'S TRIP FROM DUBLIN

It was bus'ness requir'd I'd from Dublin be straying:
    I bargained the captain to sail pretty quick;
But just at the moment the anchor was weighing,
    A spalpeen he wanted to play me a trick.
Says he, 'Paddy, go down stairs, and fetch me some beer, now.'
    Says I, 'By my shoul, you're monstratiously kind:
Then you'll sail away, and I'll look mighty queer, now,
    When I come up and see myself all left behind.'

        Chorus:
    With my tal de ral lal de ral lal de ral la ral la tal de ral la ral la, la
        tal la la;
    And sing pal li luh, whil li luh, whil li luh, pal li, luh,
    Whack, botheration, and langolee.

A storm met the ship, and did so mightily dodge her,
    Says the captain, 'We'll sink, or be all cast away,'
Thinks I, 'Never mind, 'cause I'm only a lodger,
    And my life is insur'd, – so the office must pay.'
But a taef who was sea-sick kick'd up such a riot,
    Though I lay quite sea-sick and speechless, poor elf,
I could not help bawling, 'You spalpeen, be quiet!
    Do you think that there's nobody dead but yourself?'

Well, we got safe on shore, ev'ry son of his mother;
    There I found an old friend, Mr. Paddy Macgee:
'Och, Dermot,' says he, 'is it you or your brother?'
    Says I, 'I've a mighty great notion it's me.'
Then I told him the bull we had made of our journey;
    But for bull-making Irishmen always bear blame;
Says he, 'My good friend, though we've bulls in Hibernia,
    They've cuckolds in England, and that's all the same.'

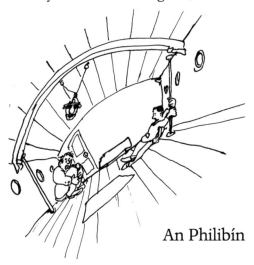

An Philibín

An Philibín ('The Lapwing') was the pseudonym of John Hackett Pollock (1897–1964), a Dublin pathologist and all-round literary man, who was a founding member of the Gate Theatre. This odd, though suitably fishy, exercise appeared in his 1957 volume of verse, Autumn Crocus. (Its Latin title must mean 'in miniature' here – it should actually mean 'in secret'.)

IN PETTO

    Being quit of pride,
I walked beside the running tide
    By Malahide;

In the wind's lull
I watched the glutton herring gull,
  With bill chock-full

Of cockle, soar,
And drop it to the stony shore
  A full half-score

Of times, to break
The shell, and, with rapacious beak,
  His breakfast take;

And when I stopped,
And stooped, to tie my lace, he dropped
  It, so it hopped

On my bald pate;
Thought I – historians relate
  The tragic fate

Of Aeschylus,
Eagle and tortoise, somewhat thus;
  Ridiculous—
    As if it mattered!

My thick calvareum's not shattered,
  But only spattered

With scollop slime—
Due meed for my degenerate time
  And feeble rhyme.

Anonymous

Dr Andrew Carpenter, editor of the pioneer anthology Verse in English
from Eighteenth-Century Ireland *(Cork University Press, 1998), from
which these spicy verses are gratefully borrowed, remarks in his illuminating
notes that in the mid-century, Stoneybatter (the current spelling of the old
road leading north-west out of the city) was notorious for its loose women.
In verse two, he further explains, a 'cully' means a man who can be duped by
a woman, 'splinters' is money and a 'bully' is a pimp.*

THE RAKES OF STONY BATTER

Come all you roving blades, that ramble thro' the City,
Kissing pretty Maids, listen to my Ditty,
Our time is coming on, when we will be merry,
Kitty, Poll, and Nan, will give us Sack and Sherry.

    Chorus:
  Hey for Bobbin Joan, Hey for Stony Batter,
  Keep your Wife at home or else I will be at her.

There's Bridget, Peg and Nell, with Nancy, Doll, & Susan,
To please their sweethearts well, sometimes will go a boozing,
But when their cash is gone, they'll hunt for a Cully,
And bring the Splinters home, to their beloved Bully.

In Summer Lasses go, to the Fields a Maying,
Thro' the Meadows gay, with their Sweethearts playing,
Their smiling winning ways, shew for game they're willing,
Tho' Jenny cries 'Nay, I won't F—k for a shilling.'

'Go you cunning Knave, no more of coax nor wheedle,

By those Buttons in my Sleeve, I'll prick you with my needle,
What will you still be bold, Mammy call to this Man,
For shame my hands don't hold, I vow my breath is just gone.'

There's Joan a buxom Lass, met with lusty Johnny,
They went to take a glass, he call'd her dear and honey,
She said 'You silly Clown, take me round the middle,
Play me Bobbin Joan, or else I'll break your fiddle.'

He gently laid her down, and he pull'd out
    his scraper,
He play'd her such a tune, which made her
    fart and caper;
She said 'My dearest John, you're such a
    jolly rover,
My cloak and gown I'll pawn, that you
    would ne'er give over.'

Come let us take a roam, up to Stony Batter,
Keep your Wife at home, for humpers will
    be at her,
Hey for cakes and ale, Hey for pretty misses,
That will never fail, for to crown our wishes.

Final Chorus:
Hey for Bobbin Joan, Hey for Stony
    Batter,
Keep your Wife at home or else I'll
    stop her water.
Is your apples ripe, are they fit for
    plucking,
Is your Maid within, ready for the
    F———g?

Anonymous

The stories and legends surrounding St Patrick's life, and particularly his celebrated banishment of the snakes from Ireland, must have given rise to literally hundreds of poetical compositions of various sorts. This one was found in a volume compiled in London by Robert Blakey, A Collection of Complete Lyrics for 200+ Songs Related to Angling (c.1855), where we learn that the lines first saw the light in Trinity College Dublin, in 1810.

SAINT PATRICK

No doubt, St Patrick was an Angler
Of credit and renown, Sir,
And many a shining trout he caught,
Ere he built Dublin town, Sir.
Old story says (it tells no lies)
He fish'd with bait and line, Sir,
At every throw he had a bite,
Which tugg'd and shook the twine, Sir.

In troubled streams he lov'd to fish,
Then salmon could not see, Sir,
The trout, and eels, and also
    pike,
Were under this decree, Sir,
And this, perhaps, may solve
    a point
With other learn'd matters, Sir,
Why Irishmen still love to fish
Among troubled waters, Sir.

Some likewise say, and even sware,
He was a godly saint, Sir,
And made 'loose fish' for all the land,
And trout as red as paint, Sir.
And as a relic of his power,
It was his ardent wish, Sir,
That dear old Erin should always have
A number of 'odd fish', Sir.

We cannot resist adding a few more Patrick-related lines here. The follow-ing memorably inept couplets have been extracted from a translation by the Rev. William Dunkin (1709?–65) of Latin verses ascribed to a medieval Irish divine, Donat or Donatus. Dunkin had a fine mastery of the cliché: typically, he uses Ireland's old and more poetic name, 'Scotia'.

'FAR WESTWARD'

Far westward lies an isle of ancient fame,
By nature bless'd, and Scotia is her name—
Enroll'd in books – exhaustless is her store
Of veiny silver and of golden ore.
Her fruitful soil forever teems with wealth;
With gems her waters, and her air with health;
Her verdant fields with milk and honey flow;
Her woolly fleeces vie with virgin snow;
Her waving furrows float with bearded corn;
Her arms and arts her envied sons adorn.
No savage bear with lawless fury roves;
No rav'ning lion through her sacred groves;
No poison there infects – no scaly snake
Creeps through the grass, nor frogs annoy the lake;—
An Ireland worthy of its pious race,
In war triumphant, and unmatched in peace.

Anonymous

There cannot be many surviving copies of The Jovial Songster: Being a Collection of Humorous Songs for the Present Year, *a cheap pamphlet published in 1805 by Thomas Ritson, Bookseller, 6 Golden-Lane, Dublin. It is full of interesting things, not the least of which is the appreciative note at the end of the one in the National Library of Ireland, which reads, in the early nineteenth-century handwriting of a previous owner:*

> *Whoever wrote it, done it well*
> *for the same is written on the Gates of Hell.*

'Sall of Copper-Alley', which appears in its pages, is a colourful snapshot of the hand-to-mouth existence of many Dubliners at the time. Close to the edge of complete penury, these are people for whom conventional morality is a luxury. They snap up anything they can get from more prosperous citizens, however it may come – a discarded wig, for example, is ideal for polishing shoes. And good meat and fish is the best thing of all.

SALL OF COPPER-ALLEY
Air: Lillies of the Valley

As I sallied forth from Essex-Bridge,
    Through many a street and lane,
With blackball, brushes and old wig,
    I sing out, Shoes To Clean.
In all my rounds I ne'er can meet
    A girl like big fat Sally,
That rubs and scrubs, and dishes wash,
That rubs and scrubs, and dishes wash,
    For Walsh in Copper-Alley;
That rubs and scrubs, and dishes wash,
    For Walsh in Copper-Alley.

When neatly tipping boots and shoes,
    Or playing pitch and toss;
Or sometimes crying, Bloody News,
    Should I chance to meet my lass,
Her pockets stuff'd with fat and lean,
    She empties in my basket;
Then off I mill to Garden-Lane,
Then off I mill to Garden-Lane,
    Where I sort my precious casket;
Then off I mill to Garden-Lane,
    Where I sort my precious casket.

On fast-days, if you should pass by,
    Ah, what a sight, ye gods;
When you her greasy fists espy,
    Hand'ling thumping cods;
She slaps the cods into her can
    Where they fit like bakers tallies;
For none their business understands,
For none their business understands,
    Like Sall of Copper-Alley;
For none their business understands,
    Like Sall of Copper-Alley.

97

Anonymous

Sandymount Strand appears in the work of writers as eminent as James Joyce and Seamus Heaney. Naturally, there were others before them who appreciated this huge empty beach lying less than three miles from the centre of the city. In October 1881 Pat printed this delightfully comprehensive paean of praise to its attractions.

SANDYMOUNT STRAND

Oh! talk not to me of your lands by the sea,
    Or of far-away Eastern shores,
Nor tell me to go to the mountains of snow,
    Where the thundering avalanche roars.
No; I'll stay if you please and enjoy the sweet breeze,
    Blowing fresh over oceans of sand,
While cockles I'll pick with a bit of a stick,
    Unbooted on Sandymount Strand.

Then wherefore describe any dusky-hair tribe,
    Or sun-frizzled 'Araby's daughter,'
When we see lovely girls with hair out of curls
    In Sandymount revel in water.
And you needn't tell me, that elsewhere in the sea,
    There are herrings one quarter as grand,
As the fat ones that glide in along with the tide
    To dine upon Sandymount Strand.

Don't rant of the powers of your forts or your towers,
    For our Pigeon House deems it insane;
Sure Martello would rise with disgusted surprise
    At comparison odious and vain.

Don't talk of the charms of old war's loud alarms,
    Or hundred-ton weapons so grand;
We'd beat the whole lot with a practising shot
    From the guns upon Sandymount Strand.

Then as to the view, why I'll prove it to you,
    If you come any sunshiny day,
That there's nothing so fine, from Ringsend to the Rhine,
    As the Sandymount side of the Bay.
Away to the right there's a beautiful sight
    In Howth's pretty mountainous land,
While front, side and rere, there's a scene just as fair,
    When you're out upon Sandymount Strand.

And some time ago we'd a capital show,
    When the band used to play at
        the tower;

The people from town, all enjoyed
    coming down,
        To promenade round for an hour.
But now they don't come, for the music
    is dumb,
        Deserted and dull is the stand;

There's nothing heard save the low sigh of the wave,
    As it falls upon Sandymount Strand.

All Dubliners know it's the best place to go
    In mental or physical pain;
To the bride 'tis content, if the honeymoon's spent
    Where in Sandymount 'surges the main,'
Now it must be confessed, I consider it best,
    When our 'Home Manufacture' is planned,
That they bear well in mind we've a capital find
    Of cockles on Sandymount Strand!

Dorothy L. Sayers

Before embarking on her masterly translation of Dante's Divine Comedy, *the English detective story writer Dorothy L. Sayers (1893–1957) served her apprenticeship as a poet by issuing two books of her own work soon after she came down from Oxford with her first-class degree. Her skills were then harnessed by the copywriting firm of S.H. Benson, where she was a fixture for the whole of the 1920s. Benson's were running the advertising campaign for Guinness at the time … and it was their bluestocking poet who came up with the stout-loving toucan, still a familiar figure today.*

'IF …'

If he can say as you can
Guinness is good for you
How grand to be a Toucan
Just think what Toucan do.

George Bernard Shaw

After leaving Dublin in 1876, Bernard Shaw (1856–1950) had no great wish to return. When in the 1930s he was asked to address the College Historical Society in Trinity, he replied with a postcard to the effect that if he felt like going anywhere (which he didn't), Ireland would be the last place he would go. If he happened to be in the country already, a visit to Dublin would be bottom of his list. Should he somehow find himself in Dublin, Trinity College would not be on his itinerary. And finally, if for some reason he went to Trinity after all, he would make very sure to avoid the College Historical Society. With regret, therefore, he was going to have to decline their kind invitation.

Despite the generous legacy he left to the National Gallery of Ireland, sentimental attachment to his native land was clearly not one of the playwright's most notable characteristics. This is graphically illustrated in the following fragment of Shavian doggerel (whose original source, incidentally, eludes us).

'AT LAST I WENT TO IRELAND'

At last I went to Ireland.
　'Twas raining cats and dogs:

　　I found no music in the glens,
　　　Nor purple in the bogs.

　　　And as for angels' laughter in
　　　　The smelly Liffey's tide—

　　　　Well, my Irish daddy said it,
　　　　　But the dear old humbug lied.

Thomas Sheridan

Remembered today largely for his close friendship with Jonathan Swift, and because he was the ancestor of a surprising number of Irish writers, Thomas Sheridan (1687–1738) made many scholarly translations of classical works, an activity befitting his calling as a cleric and schoolmaster. He also generated a paper snowstorm of far less respectable songs, squibs, apophthegms and anagrams, some of which appeared in the Dublin prints of the time. However, few were published in book form until Robert Hogan's The Poems of Thomas Sheridan *came out in 1994. The three examples below of his work come from that exemplary collection. They demonstrate that Walter Scott hit the mark when he called him 'the good-natured, light-hearted and ingenious Sheridan'.*

'The Tale of the T—d', as the title coyly put it on first publication – probably in 1728 – is a pungent but truly moral tale, whose imagery is justified by the stinging message it delivers to all 'upstart scoundrels'.

THE TALE OF THE T[UR]D

A pastry-cook once moulded up a t—d
(You may believe me when I give my word)
With nice ingredients of the fragrant kind
And sugar of the best, right doubl' refined.
He blends them all, for he was fully bent
Quite to annihilate its taste and scent.
With outstretched arms, he twirls the rolling-pin,
And spreads the yielding ordure smooth and thin
'Twas not to save his flour, but show his art,
Of such foul dough to make a sav'ry tart.
He heats his ov'n with care, and baked it well,
But still the crust's offensive to the smell;
The cook was vexed to see himself so soiled,
So works it to a dumpling, which he boiled;

Now out it comes, and if it stunk before,
It stinks full twenty times as much, and more.
He breaks fresh eggs, converts it into batter,
Works them with spoon about a wooden platter,
To true consistence, such as cook-maids make
At Shrovetide, when they toss the pliant cake.
In vain he twirls the pan; the more it fries,
The more the nauseous, fetid vapors rise.
Resolved to make it still a sav'ry bit,
He takes the pancake, rolls it round a spit,
Winds up the jack, and sets it to the fire;
But roasting raised its pois'nous fumes the high'r.
Offended much (although it was his own),
At length he throws it where it should be thrown;

And in a passion, storming loud, he cried,
'If neither baked, nor boiled, nor roast, nor fried,
Can thy offensive, hellish taint reclaim,
Go to the filthy jake from whence you came.'

The Moral

This tale requires but one short application:
It fits all upstart scoundrels in each nation,
Minions of fortune, wise men's jest in pow'r,
Like weeds on dunghills, stinking, rank and sour.

*After that, you might hesitate if invited to dinner by the Rev. Thomas Sheridan.
But you would surely go in the end, and you would enjoy yourself there.*

'AN INVITATION'

I send this at nine
To know will you dine
On a beefsteak of mine.
As I'm a divine
I'll give you good wine,
Old, gen'rous and fine.
Till death I am thine,
Thomas Sheridine.

This final verse appeared in Faulkner's Dublin Journal, 21–25 January 1734,
*and may not be by the irrepressible Thomas Sheridan at all. Robert Hogan
consigns it to a section of his book called 'Poems of Doubtful Attribution' – a
measure of how difficult it was to pin down the man's literary legacy. But
whoever wrote it, the heartfelt couplet deserves its place in this company.*

ON THE REVD DR SWIFT, D.S.P.D. LEAVING HIS FORTUNE TO BUILD AN HOSPITAL FOR IDIOTS AND LUNATICS

The Dean must die? – Our idiots to maintain!
Perish ye idiots! – and long live the Dean!

Daragh Smith

Oliver Gogarty's bawdry is still read, but less well-known are the improper verses written in the 1930s by a young Dublin doctor, Daragh Smith. For half a century these were passed on verbally in medical circles, often in garbled form, until the enterprising Eoin O'Brien, of the Black Cat Press, persuaded the author to allow him to issue a selection in the 1980s. This limited edition, entitled Dissecting Room Ballads from the Dublin Schools of Medicine 50 Years Ago, *and a small reprint in 1992, are now both collector's items.*

THE SEA BABOON

Oh why are the wild waves
    fleckt wi' blood
And the sea shore stained
    with red?
Oh hark! The Tale of the Sea
    Baboon—
The tale of a race now dead!

The last of his race was the
    Sea Baboon,
Huge, and black with an oily
    skin,

And his penis pink and his foreskin too
Had an undulant dorsal fin.

Of a sudden a thought struck the Sea Baboon
And he closed his jaws with a snap!
And he looked at his balls – his hairy balls
Like a bear curled up in his lap.

And then into the sea dashed the Sea Baboon,
Lust passion had entered his soul
For spring had come to that solitary beast
And he longed, yes he longed – for his Hole!

A female shark came swimming along
A quiet elderly dame
And he ambled up and accosted her
With never a thought of shame!

And he caught her tail as
    she whisked away
(Oh vile, unnatural crime!)
She yielded, and there on
    the ocean bed
They worked away for a time.

This served to whet his appetite—
He next had a slim young whale;
Then a couple more sharks and as yet no sign
Of his prowess beginning to fail.

Look! What is that slim and graceful form?
That alluring shade of grey!
'We'll have one more' says the Sea Baboon
'Then we'll chuck it and call it a day.'

But alas, the submarine, U.6.3.
Its propeller whirrs apace!
And it cut off the balls of the Sea Baboon
The last pair of *BALLS* in the *RACE*.

BRIAN BORU'S FRENCH LETTER

I was up to my oxters in turf mould
At my contract down in the bog
When my slane chanced to strike against something
Like a stone, or a lump of a log.

'Twas a box of the finest bogoak, Sir
And I wondered just what it might hide
So I muttered 'Well – bugger the fairies!'
And I took a wee look, Sir, inside.

I suppose now, you'll scarcely believe me
It's almost too good to be true
'Twas an *Ancient Irish French Letter*
A relic of Brian Boru!

'Twas an ancient Irish
    French letter
Made of elk skin, and
    just a foot tall.
And a little gold tag
    at the bottom
Gave his name, and his
    stud fee, and all.

And my mind flittered back through the ages
To the time of that sturdy old Celt.
There was Granuaile up on the bedstead
And Brian Boru in his pelt.

And I heard him remark rather firmly
Listen here now, we must get this right
Though you did have your own way last night Dear
IT'S THE HAIRY SIDE OUTWARDS TONIGHT.

Colin Smythe

A winning Yeats parody published in TCD Miscellany *in the 1960s, when the writer was an undergraduate. As an independent publisher, Colin Smythe continues to render sterling service to the shades of Yeats and his circle (and to Irish literature in general) by issuing many scholarly works by and about them.*

ODE TO SALLY GARDINER

Down in the College Buttery my love and I did meet,
She was seated by herself 'pon a little purple seat.
She bid me take some coffee, ''Tis made here instantly',
But I being wise and learnèd with her would not agree.

In a queue by the counter my love and I did stand.
She leaned upon my shoulder as we stood there hand in hand.
She bid me take life slowly, 'We shall be here for years',
But I was damned impatient and left her to her tears.

Anonymous

The last of our selections from the 'Lyra Liffeiana' series from Pat. *This one, published on 6 August 1881, takes the form of a sort of urban* aisling, *or alluring supernatural vision. The poet modestly dedicated his verses to 'The Dublin Ladies'.*

THE SONG OF THE LIFFEY SPRITE

I still maintain I wasn't tight,
    Although I'd been to dinner;
But once returning late at night,
    Like any other sinner,
I saw on Carlisle Bridge a form,
    And knew it was a fairy;
For, though the weather wasn't warm,
    Her clothes were light and airy.

A plenitude of leg was seen
    (I thought it most improper);
But then she was a fairy queen
    (And so one couldn't stop her)—
Just like an ancient statue, or
    A 'lady of the ballet'—
I shorten my descriptions, for
    I'm very prone to dally.

The time was only half-past one—
    I heard the half-hour ringing;
But even ere the chimes were done
    The spirit started singing.
She sang of things that come and go,
    Of summers and of swallows,

Of sums of money, sailors, snow,
    And then went on as follows:—

'Behold in me the guardian sprite
    Of Dublin's dirty city,
Where cars are cheap and pockets light,
    And all the women pretty;
But Dublin's sons are stern and hard;
    They every one despise her;
She hasn't got a single bard
    Who will immortalize her.'

And as the words were said to me,
    Although I'm not a Rousseau,
A Locker, Calverly, or Leigh,
    I thought I'd try to do so;
So there you are, fair reader – now
    (I thought you'd like to know it),
I've done my best to tell you how
    I first became a poet.

Anonymous

Sometimes, though not often, a song lyric crosses the open border between everyday verse and true poetry. 'The Spanish Lady', a moving chronicle of doomed erotic obsession that was written some time in the second half of the nineteenth century, certainly achieves this.

In the fourth verse, a 'mot' is a girlfriend or mistress, while a 'swaddy' is a slang term for a soldier or ex-soldier – though the 'puddle swaddy' here may simply be a veteran of Dublin's muddy streets, a 'gurrier' or 'cornerboy'. In Ireland, the 'Provost Marshall' was an important officer with both military and policing responsibilities.

THE SPANISH LADY

As I went out through Dublin City
At the hour of twelve o'clock of the night,
Who should I see but a Spanish lady
Washing her feet by candlelight.
First she washed them and then she dried them,
Over a fire of ambry coals—
In all my life I never did see
A maid so sweet about the soles.

I stopped to look but the watchman passed,
Says he, 'Young fellow, the night is late.
Along with you home or I will wrestle you
Straight away through the Bridewell gate.'
I threw a look to the Spanish lady,
Hot as the fire of ambry coals—
In all my life I ne'er did see
Such a maid so neat about the
    soles.

As I walked back through
    Dublin City
As the dawn of day was o'er,
Who should I see but the
    Spanish lady
When I was weary and
    footsore.
She had a heart so filled
    with loving
And her love she longed to share—
In all my life I never did meet
With a maid who had so much
    to spare.

113

Now she's no mot for a puddle swaddy
With her ivory comb and her mantle so fine,
But she'd make a wife for the Provost Marshall
Drunk on brandy and claret wine.
I got a look from the Spanish lady
Hot as a fire of ambry coals—
In all my life I never did meet
With a maid so neat about the soles.

I've wandered north and I've wandered south
By Stoney Batter and Patrick's Close,
Up and around by the Gloucester Diamond
And back by Napper Tandy's house.
Old age has laid her hand upon me
Cold as a fire of ashy coals—
But where is the lonely Spanish lady
Neat and sweet about the soles?

As I was leaving Dublin City
On that morning sad of heart,
Lonely was I for the Spanish lady
Now that forever we must part.
But still I always will remember
All the hours we did enjoy—
But then she left me sad at parting;
Gone forever was my joy.

Anonymous

Occasionally a Dublin saleroom will announce a sale of 'Literary and Historical Collectables'. This one offers a cornucopia of curiosities from the mid-nineteenth century and before. Some come from real life, like the natural phenomenon of the 'moving bog', Edmund Kean's famous stage cloak, Paganini's long musical nose, or the noisily articulated wooden leg of the First Marquess of Anglesey (made to replace the one buried with full military honours near Waterloo). Others lots come from songs – King O'Toole's gander and the button from Paddy Hegarty's breeches can both be found in Ireland's Other Poetry, *while Jemmy O'Brien is hanged on page 64 of the present book. In a broadsheet ballad called 'Bishop M'Cue or, the Charity Sermon', we discover that the episcopal blister of the final verse is a sort of booby-trap poultice that causes his Lordship to rip off his robes in the pulpit, shouting, 'Beelzebub's in my breeches!'*

Mysteries remain, of course, and your suggestions are welcome. What precisely happened to Darby Kenny? When was Tommy Galvin a hangman, and could the man with the plaid cloak be the despised Major Sirr – whose own collection of curios was purchased by the Royal Irish Academy? Most puzzling of all – who was Stoney Pocket himself?

The verses are taken from an undated collection, The Dublin Comic Songster: A Selection of the Most Fashionable Comic Songs.

STONEY POCKET'S AUCTION
Air: 'Umbrella Courtship.'

Gentlemen, we'll soon begin,
    There are seats for those that walk in,
And goods well worth your notice here,
    At Stoney Pocket's auction:
If you have an antiquarian taste,
    You'll just step in and see 'em—
Don't miss this opportunity
    Of filling your museum.

But if I cannot coax,
    I'll call the catalogue, sirs,
The article marked No. 1,

Is piece of the moving bog, sirs;
No. 2, is in the hall,
   Nailed up in one of the niches,
It's the flap and ivory button
   Of Paddy Hegarty's breeches.

No. 3, is a telescope,
   Blind Homer bought to gaze with,
No. 4, is the piece of chalk,
   That Shakspere wrote his plays with.
No. 5, is the gander's neck,
   Belonging to King O'Toole, sirs,
And we've the rotten crock that smothered
   Darby Kenny with the goold, sirs.

We have lots of books that printed was
   Before the world began, sirs,
And written in a language
   That was never spoke by man, sirs.
In the glass-case, No. 9,
   Is two small things stitched together.
Those are the lips of Jemmy O'Brien,
   That's worn with *smacking leather*.

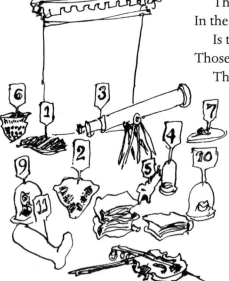

We have Lord Anglesey's old wooden leg,
    He hopped from Waterloo on,
It's made of piece of an apple-tree,
    That oysters often grew on;
You will also see a splendid cloak,
    Was worn by Kean, the stager,
And the plaid one hanging next to that,
    Was worn by the Major.

If there's any boys from Wicklow here,
    The time they'll surely nick, sirs,
As the Auctioneer is knocking down,
    The kippeen of a stick, sirs;
Musicians too may have a treat,
    If they wish to sport a guinea.
They can buy the string, the bow and bridge,
    Of the nose of Paganini.

To stop the mouth of a scolding wife,
    Buy Bishop M'Cue's fine blister,
And to hang her we have a good ropes-end,
    Tommy Galvin's wizen twister!
There are other goods whose names are far
    Too numerous to be told, sirs,
But to-morrow night I'll call them out,
    If they're not already sold, sirs.

Jonathan Swift

One Sunday morning, reports Dr Patrick Delaney in his Observations *(1754),
the organist Tom Roseingrave, just back from Italy and 'far gone in the Ital-
ian taste', played a voluntary in St Patrick's Cathedral. This so impressed
Dean Swift (1667–1745) that, despite being almost tone-deaf, he was able to
reproduce impromptu 'a most ridiculous and droll imitation' of it that night
at the dinner-table. The great man's nonsense words were promptly written
down and eventually published in Falkiner's collected edition, complete with
the music that inspired them.*

CANTATA

In Harmony would you Excel
Suit your Words to your Musick well,
Musick well, Musick well,
Suit your Words to your Musick well,
Suit your Words to your Musick well.

For Pegasus runs runs every Race
By Galloping high or Level Pace,
Or Ambling or Sweet Canterbury
Or with a down a high down derry.

No, no Victory Victory he ever got
By Jogling Jogling Jogling trot.
No Muse harmonious Entertains,
Rough Roystring Rustick Roaring Strains,
Nor shall you twine the Crackling Crackling Bays
By Sneaking, Sniv'lling Round Delays.

Now slowly move your Fiddle Stick,
Now tan tan tan tan tan tan tivi,
Now tan tan tan tan tan tan tivi quick,

Quick now, Trembling, Shiv'ring, Quiv'ring, Quaking,
Set hoping, hoping, hoping hearts of Lovers akeing.
   Fly, fly
   Above the Sky,
   Rambling, Gambling,
   Rambling, Gambling,
Trolloping, Lolloping, Galloping
Trolloping, Lolloping, Galloping,
   Trollop, Lollop, Trollop, Gallop,
   Lollop, Trollop, Gallop, Lollop.
   Now Creep, Sweep,
       Sweep, Sweep the deep.
       See!
         See!
          Celia Celia dies,
            Dies, Dies, Dies,
              Dies, Dies, Dies,

      While true Lovers' Eyes
    Weeping Sleep, Sleeping Weep, Weeping Sleep.
Bo Peep, Bo Peep, Bo Peep, Bo Peep,
Bo Peep, Bo Peep, Peep, Bo Bo Peep!

Swift was invited to dinner. As the story goes, when he entered the dining room he detected a nasty smell of meat that had been allowed to go off in the warm weather. When asked to say grace, he intoned:

DEAN SWIFT'S GRACE

O God on high
Look down from the sky
And bless this leg of mutton,
And give us meat
That we can eat
For this meat here is rotten.

In his delightful book, Life on the Liffey, *the late John O'Donovan suggested that Swift was probably the writer of the following quatrain about the editor of a Dublin scandal-sheet called* Whalley's News Letter. *It seems that John Whalley (1653–1724) was a fine fellow indeed, 'a shoemaker who diversified into quack medicine, necromancy, astrology and yellow journalism'.*

'EPITAPH ON JOHN WHALLEY'

Here five foot deep lies on his back
A cobbler, starmonger, and quack,
Who to the stars in pure good will
Does to his best look upward still.

Anonymous

A deliciously silly account, which one suspects may be largely true, of what happened after three convivial Trinity students thought of sheltering in the Sandymount Martello Tower. From TCD Miscellany, 9 November 1951.

THREE BLIND MICE

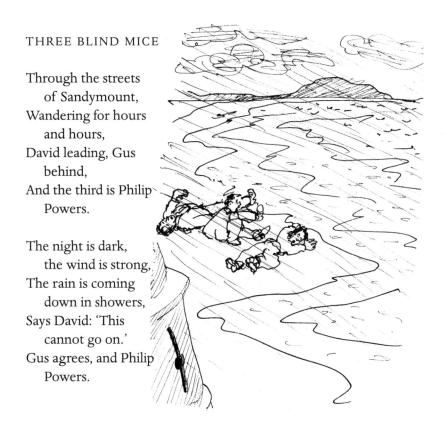

Through the streets
   of Sandymount,
Wandering for hours
   and hours,
David leading, Gus
   behind,
And the third is Philip
   Powers.

The night is dark,
   the wind is strong,
The rain is coming
   down in showers,
Says David: 'This
   cannot go on.'
Gus agrees, and Philip
   Powers.

So the merry travellers three,
Seeing six Martello Towers,
Mount the wall that bounds the sea,
David, Gus, and Philip Powers.

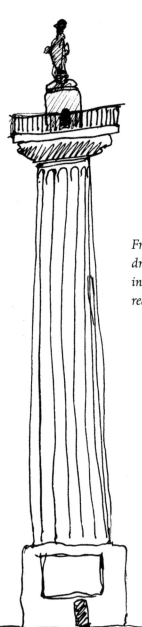

Out into the air they jump
(Maidens, gather wreaths of flowers),
Upon the sand they fall ker-rump,
David, Gus, and Philip Powers.

Socialites, by this be warned,
Avoid pink gins and whiskey sours,
Or you will meet an awful fate
Like David, Gus, and Philip Powers.

Anonymous

From Dublin Opinion, *August 1928. One of hundreds, perhaps thousands, of short verses published in the magazine over the years. For some reason it reduced both editors of this volume to jellies.*

THRILLER

There was a young fellow named Spiller,
Who fell from the top of the Pillar,
    And remarked as he fell:
    'It's the distance as well
As the jolly old pace that's a killer.'

J.G.C. Trench

The last of our 'Guinness' verses here. In 1956 this one achieved the rare accolade (for an advertisment) of being included in a Penguin anthology, More Comic and Curious Verse, *edited by J.M. Cohen.*

THE SENSIBLE SEA-LION

The sea-lion, naturalists disclose,
Can balance balls upon his nose,
And some, so neatly does he judge it,
Ask, 'If a ball, why not a budget?'
No head for figures is his knob—
His eye's not on the Chancellor's job.
He doesn't balance gains with losses,
But pleasure on his own proboscis.
And rightly, he prefers to win his
Spurs by demonstrating Guinness.
Perhaps this very session he'll
Be chosen as Lord Privy Seal.

Anonymous

These lines, which may be funnier than they were intended to be, were also written as an advertisement, for the Dublin firm of brush manufacturers. They appeared in Dublin Opinion *during its first year of publication, 1922.*

VARIAN'S BRUSHES

From the dawning of the day
   Until evening sunset flushes
Every hour and every way
   There's a use for Varian's Brushes.

The clouds may sweep across the sun,
   The wind may sweep across the rushes,
But if sweeping's to be done
   There's nothing up to Varian's Brushes.

R.P. Weston and F.J. Barnes

This touching ditty from the British music-hall tradition was issued in 1909 by the firm of Francis, Day and Hunter, Ltd. Our inexhaustive research has failed to uncover any details of the song's composers: the picture they paint of this Dubliner in foreign parts is a far cry from the traditional portrait of the 'Exile from Erin'.

I'VE GOT RINGS ON MY FINGERS

Now Jim O'Shea was cast away
Upon an Indian Isle.
The natives there they liked his hair,
They liked his Irish smile,
So made him chief Panjandrum,
The Nabob of them all.
They called him Jij-ji-boo Jhai,
And rigged him out so gay,
So he wrote to Dublin Bay,
To his sweetheart, just to say:

Chorus:
  Sure, I've got rings on my fingers, bells on my toes,
  Elephants to ride upon, my little Irish Rose;
  So come to your Nabob, and next Patrick's Day,
  Be Mistress Mumbo Jumbo Jij-ji-boo J. O'Shea.

Across the sea went Rose Magee
To see her Nabob grand.
He sat within his palanquin,
And when she kissed his hand,
He led her to his harem,
Where he had wives galore.
She started shedding a tear;
Said he, 'Now have no fear,
I'm keeping these wives here
Just for ornament, my dear.'

In emerald green he robed his
    queen,
To share with him his throne.
'Mid eastern charms and
    waving palms
They'd shamrocks, Irish grown,
Sent all the way from Dublin
To Nabob J. O'Shea
But in his palace so fine
Should Rose for Ireland pine,
With smiles her face will shine
When he murmurs, 'Sweet-
    heart mine'.

Terence de Vere White

In the 1960s he was literary editor of the Irish Times, *but the novelist and biographer Terence de Vere White (1912–94) published his first writings in the 1920s, under the pseudonym of 'Edelweiss'. This* jeu d'esprit *appeared in* The College Pen, *a TCD undergraduate magazine, on Guy Fawkes' Day, 1929. It concerns a rite of passage from those supposedly more innocent times – when Trinity set more exams than it does today. The altogether admirable 'Little-go', for example, a general test in the humanities, had to be passed even by students who were doing science. But there were other, more intimate, peaks to conquer too.*

ONWARDS

Entering with an exhibition,
Johnny gave up Prohibition,
Went dancing with the greatest haste,
Placed an arm about her waist.

How the march of time goes on,
Junior Fresh. is passed and gone,
Johnny at the pictures put
His large upon her little foot.

Little-go presents no qualms
To a man of Johnny's charms,
Down the town he gaily skips,
Plants a kiss upon her lips.

Still remains some crowns to win,
Ambition is a grievous sin,
Cries the lady: 'Please keep off,'
Said John: 'I am a Junior Soph.'

Now on a horse-hair sofa red,
Johnny smiled and then he said,
As he placed her on his knee,
   'I have gained my Arts Degree.'

Anonymous

In that curious volume of satirical verses, Secret Springs of Dublin Song *(1918), the only contributor to appear by name is Susan Mitchell, who wrote the introduction. The following poem is most probably the work of Seamus O'Sullivan (1879–1958). While it remains open to speculation as to who the canine in question is supposed to represent, the obvious candidate must be W.B. Yeats, if only because of his 1910 squib, 'To a Poet, who would have me Praise certain Bad Poets, Imitators of His and Mine'. That concludes with the celebrated line: 'But was there ever dog that praised his fleas?'*

Though crowds once gathered if I raised my hand,
I have grown now to be like that old swan
That, lonely, swimming, frowns the summer through
Because he finds his voice inadequate;
Or that he must so constantly seek out
The base intruders that have built their nests
In difficult places under his wings.

Richard D'Alton Williams

In 1848 John Mitchel was arrested and his revolutionary newspaper suppressed, so his friend Richard D'Alton Williams (1822–62), a regular of Thomas Davis's journal, The Nation, *immediately started another one. This too was closed down, and Williams was tried for treason-felony. Mitchel had been sentenced to transportation and, as the lines below suggest, Williams might not have minded that too much himself, but his lawyer (the writer, Samuel Ferguson) managed to get him acquitted. Within three years, after qualifying as a doctor, Williams left Ireland anyway; he spent the rest of his short life in America.*

In Ireland's Other Poetry *we reproduced 'The Dream', the sixth of the poet's series of long humorous verses entitled 'Misadventures of a Medical Student'. Here we present extracts from the fourth, a typically impish piece of work that combines, as Williams did in his life, the world of medicine with that of the Irish revolutionary nationalist.*

The title simply means 'imprisoned' – i.e. 'put into quod'; the tavern near the Robinson and Bussell 'Music Warerooms' may have been Patrick Fox's 'Shell Fish Tavern' on Fleet Street; the 'epigastric muscles' are those around the stomach; the 'Natives' are Irish oysters. These and other similar details might provide material for a gripping study of Dublin life in the

1840s, but this is not the place for it. Far better to let Williams's beautifully modulated rhythms flow over you, and his meaning will seep gently into your mind.

from QUODDED

There's a tavern off Westmoreland-street, near Robinson and Bussell's,
Where I often took the wrinkles from my epigastric muscles,
And sometimes brought a friend or so right valiantly to join
In a foray on the 'Natives' or a Jousting with Sir Loin;
And oft I condescended with my solemn host to chatter
Of steam-engines and rattle-snakes, or any other matter.
I glanced at apple-dumplings, monster-meetings, civil wars,
Ham sandwiches, geology, the Oregon, the stars,
Hydropathy, the Puseyites, the newspapers, and soup,
And gave himself advice for gout, his child the same for croup.
I blarneyed him, I plastered him, I stuck it on in lumps,
I said he was a 'roarer,' and the emperor of trumps;
And I called him, while he boarded me respectably on tick,
The quintessence concentrated of a sublimated brick.

But then the poet's host and dining companion (who is also his landlord)
demands his long overdue rent. The poet reacts intemperately.

In wrath I, somewhat rashly, drew a scalpel from my pocket
To amputate his humerus directly at the socket;
But slips belong unhappily to surgery and dancing,
I stumbled on an orange-peel while hastily advancing,
And only slightly wounded, through his 'ready-made' habiliments,
Some intercostohumeralcutaneous nervous filaments;
And then he called a gentleman in deep cerulean blue,
With cabalistic symbols on his broidered collar too.

The policeman hauls away the poet. He is sent for trial for insolvency.

What! – a minstrel of the *Nation* – therefore one of 'nature's nobs'—
To be sent, with knights and aldermen, and other prosy snobs,

For malt arrears, to Jericho – although, did Guinness know it,
He'd bring me here his finest beer, and never charge a poet.

They listened to my eloquence; but yet, 'tis very odd,
They sent me ignominiously, the savages, to quod.
Farewell to Poupart's ligament, the brain, and caeliac axis,
The lancet and the tourniquet, the cannula and taxis!
Adieu St Vincent's, Dun's, the Meath, obstetrical diameters!
I'm left alone, in quod to groan, or howl my own hexameters,
And muse upon a law like this, so dolorously funny,
That takes away my liberty because I haven't money.

*But the poet has a plan – he suspects that a detective from Dublin Castle is
listening up the chimney, so he sings rebel songs and practises subversive
speeches in his cell.*

So, as I ever like to have a little quiet fun,
I sat me down beside the hob, and, having first begun
To damn the Court Insolvent for refusing my petition,
I projected up the chimney a Vesuvius of sedition;
Especially on railway wars I came it very strong,
And then I sang, extempore, a treasonable song,
Particularly lauding in the chorus of my lays
A pyrotechnic plan to set the Liffey in a blaze;
And my melody, no doubt of it, was sweet as Hybla's dew
To the tympanum detective of the 'crusher' in the flue.
And now I'm hoping constantly – I trust not without reason—
To be put upon my trial for sedition or high treason,
And thus at once win martyrdom and Richmond country air
By means of 'a delusion, a mockery, and a snare';
But it very much depends upon the Alphabetic liver
Whether he'll believe or not the quiz about the river.

The 'Alphabetic liver' belongs to the Attorney-General – who was known as 'Alphabet Smith' after the many initial letters he put before his name. If he believes the poet's terrorist hoax ('the quiz about the river') – and if the solid state of his digestion ('dura …') makes him grumpy enough – he may convict the prisoner of conspiring against the state, and send him, a fully-fledged Irish patriot at last, into a welcome exile.

Perhaps, if his digestion's good, he'll be a little sceptical,
But men will snap at anything when surly and dyspeptical.
So here I stay imploring all the consonants and vowels
To constipate imperviously the Alphabetic bowels;
And should the fates decree him 'dura ilia messorum,'
I confidently hope to stand ere long arraigned before him,
Accused of 'foul conspiracy' – God knows, perhaps to shatter
The Pigeon-House with lollypop, or capture Stoneybatter.

Zozimus
(Michael J. Moran)

No collection of 'Dublin's other poetry' could possibly be complete without a contribution from the famous blind street-singer and versifier, Zozimus – or to use his real name, Michael J. Moran (c.1796–c.1856). We have found space here for two. The first is a sort of advertisement for the poet/balladeer, his own little bit of trumpet-blowing. Perhaps he used it as a warm-up routine while people gathered around, before he launched into his performance in earnest.

THE ADDRESS OF ZOZIMUS TO HIS FRIENDS

If yez want wit and fun,
To me, Zozimus, run,
For I am the boy,
Your hope and your joy,
To enliven your sowl,
And your passions controul
With my jokes and blarney,
Like Kate of Killarney,
And her looks so charming.
If yez wish to be wise
Just open your eyes,
And read every page
Of Zozimus the sage;
For I am the lad
To make your hearts glad,
With my hook and my crook,
And my straw and my book,
I will no nonsense brook.

Ye aged and ye youth,
If you wish to have truth
On Zozimus dwell,
Who loves you so well,
I'm always at home,
Except when I'll roam,
Some kind fellows to meet
In the alley or street,
With my wife so discreet;
If you'll have humour and glee,
Be sure you'll come to me;
Come to Zozimus bold,
Who will all tales unfold,
By the night and the day.
Hear all I will say,
Both early and late,
I will give you a treat
And a new song complete.

'The Last Words of Zozimus' is also the last entry in this collection. The lines are is taken from the only book ever written about him, an unreliable little work from 1871 called Memoir of the Great Original Zozimus (Michael Moran), *put together by someone lurking under the name of Gulielmus Dubliniensis Humoriensis. A misguided attempt is made to reproduce in print the speaker's Dublin accent, with 'av' replacing 'of', 'gaynious' instead of 'genius' and so forth. This renders it all difficult and unpleasant to read, at least to our modern eyes. We therefore revert here to more standard spelling – though not for 'yees', which is still a perfectly good way of saying 'you' (plural) in Dublin.*

Seen afresh in this way, perhaps 'The Last Words of Zozimus' can be seen as the honest and moving testimony it is. He tips his hat to his most eminent friends (or patrons), the poets Samuel Lover and J.F. Waller (who founded the Dublin University Review), *the Reverend Charles Tisdall,* DD, FTCD, *and the conductor and 'Lecturer on Vocal Music', Prof. Glover. Clearly, Zozimus had no false modesty, for he goes on to measure himself against the great Tommy 'Anacreon' Moore, then probably Ireland's most celebrated writer of all.*

THE LAST WORDS OF ZOZIMUS,
IMPROVISATORE OF THAT NAME

My burying-place is no concern to me,
In the O'Connell Circle let it be—
As to my funeral; all pomp is vain,
Illustrious people does prefer it plain;
When gifted men is laid upon the shelf,
None of one's followers exceeds oneself;
I'll not attempt to trouble old or young,
Nor shall the street where Zozimus has sung
Require more guarding, as they would, of course,
From any stiff Bluebottle of the Force.

'The Poet of the People' should be borne
From whence not even Zozimus can return,
Without or pomp, or pride, or vain display—
Don't take a 'round', just move the straightest way,
Though I *was* famed in my eventful day;
One coffin and one horse is quite enough,
One mourning jingle will be *quantum suff.;*
But have enough of whiskey and of snuff,
And though convivial when in body able,
I never liked the vile dissecting table,
So have your eyes upon the Sack-em-up,
And if they stirs be pleased to trip-em-up.

I have no coronet to go before me,
Nor Bucephalius that ever bore me,
But put my hat, and stick, and gloves together,
That bore for years the very worst of weather;
And rest assured in spirit will be there,
'Mary of Egypt' and 'Susannah' fair,
And 'Pharoah's Daughter' with the heavenly blushes
That took the drowning goslin' from the rushes.

I'll not permit a tombstone stuck above me,
Nor effigy; but, boys, if still yees love me,
Build a neat house for all whose fate is hard,
And give a bed to every wanderin' bard;
If genius yees admire, I'd have yees show it
By giving pipe and porter to the Poet;
Make my respects to Waller and to Lover,
To Charley Tisdall and Professor Glover;
And if posterity is just, I'm sure
I'll be as famous as Anacreon Moore.

Our country yet will Phoenix-like revive
When neither France nor Prussia shall survive.
Yees ask me why I know of such a thing,
Or dream about what other times will bring,
It is because though blind and steeped in night
We poets has forethought and second-sight,
And prophesies the things that yet shall come
After yees shall have the blest millennium.
Now, boys – goodbye – my grave disturbs not me,
In the O'Connell Circle – let it be.

In the original title of that poem Zozimus prophesied that he would die in 1848; though his biographer says he was gone two years before that, Daniel O'Connell was still alive then, so there was of course no 'O'Connell Circle' in Glasnevin Cemetery. At least Zozimus avoided the 'Sack-em-up' grave-robbers, for his wish to be laid there (probably in 1856) was respected, and enjoyed a large funeral. Today you can still pay your respects to that irrepressible balladeer, for a monument was recently erected over his last resting-place.

W.B. Yeats once called him 'The Last Gleeman'. The compliment was meant warmly, but the recent sad death of Ronnie Drew, a true Dubliner in more than one sense, reminds us that Zozimus was far from being the last of the city's great minstrels. Echoes in words and music of all their voices look set to roll on for ever, or until the final silence descends (whichever comes first).

Acknowledgments and Thanks

The Editors and Publisher are grateful for permission to reproduce copyright material in this book, and for the generosity of copyright holders. Every effort has been made to trace copyright holders, but despite strenuous researches this has proved impossible in a few cases. The Publisher would be interested to hear from any that we have failed to locate.

Fergus Allen: 'To Trinity College 1943' and 'This Man's Meat' (both originally published in *TCD Miscellany* during the early 1940s), with thanks to the author. / Brendan Behan: 'The Old Triangle' from his play *The Quare Fellow* (Methuen 1956), with thanks to the Behan Estate. / George Bonass: 'A Ballade of the Future' from his collection *Verse or Worse* by 'P.O.P.' (Cahill & Co 1928) and 'A Stout Saint' from *The Guinness Harp* (April–May 1961). / Vincent Caprani: 'The Dubliner' and 'Gough's Statue' from his collection *Rowdy Rhymes and Rec-im-itations: Doggerel for a Departed Dublin* (1982), with thanks to the author. / Maurice James Craig: 'Kilcarty to Dublin', from his collection *Some Way for Reason* (Heinemann 1948), with thanks to the author. / Morgan Dockrell: 'Awkcents', with thanks to the author. / M.F. Egan: 'At Kingsbridge' from his *Ballade of Distraction & Other Poems* (M.H. Gill 1956). / Mick Fitzgerald: 'Me Brother is a TD', with thanks to the author. / Leslie Gillespie: 'Marching Through Georgia' from *The New Northman* (Winter 1940–41), with thanks to Elgy Gillespie. / Oliver St John Gogarty: 'The Hay Hotel' from *The Poems and Plays of Oliver St John Gogarty*, edited by A.N. Jeffares (Colin Smythe Ltd 2001), with thanks to Colin Smythe Ltd on behalf of Veronica J. O'Mara. / Bryan Guinness: 'The Axolotl', to the estate of the late Bryan Guinness. / F.R. Higgins: 'The Old Jockey', from *The Gap of Brightness* (MacMillan 1940). / 'Paul Jones': 'A Plea for Nelson Pillar' from *Fifteen Years of Dublin Opinion* (ND), 'Varian's Brushes' (Anonymous) from *Dublin Opinion* (November 1922), and 'Thriller' (Anonymous) from *Dublin Opinion* (August 1928), with thanks to the estate of the late C.E. Kelly. / Charlie Keegan: 'Ode to a Giant Snail Found in a Dublin Garden', with thanks to the author. / M.J. MacManus: 'Remembrance' from his *Dublin Diversions* (Talbot Press 1928), and 'Eden Quay' and 'A Lament for the Days that are Gone' from his *A Green Jackdaw: Adventures in Parody* (Talbot Press 1939), with thanks to the estate of the late M.J. MacManus. / Liam O'Meara: 'Moving Statues', with thanks to the author. / Dorothy L. Sayers: 'If ...'

from *The Book of Guinness Advertising*, by Brian Sibley (Guinness Superlatives 1980), 'Enquiring Edward' (Anonymous) from *National Student* (January–February 1939) and *The Sensible Sea-Lion* by J.G.C. Trench from *More Comic and Curious Verse*, edited by J.M. Cohen (Penguin Books 1956), to Guinness Superlatives. / George Bernard Shaw: 'At Last I Went to Ireland', with thanks to the Society of Authors, on behalf of the Estate of Bernard Shaw. / Daragh Smith: 'Brian Boru's French Letter' and 'The Sea Baboon' from his *Dissecting Room Ballads from the Dublin Schools of Medicine 50 Years Ago* (Black Cat Press 1992), with thanks to Eoin O'Brien. / Colin Smythe: 'Ode to Sally Gardiner', with thanks to the author. / Terence De Vere White: 'Onwards' from *The College Pen* (5 November 1929), with thanks to Victoria Glendinning.

We are also grateful for many other kindnesses to the following, who helped us in various ways during the preparation of this work: Fergus Allen, Peter and Mary Costello, Maurice Craig, Jeremy Crow, Joseph Ledwidge, Julie Moller, Constantine Normanby, Liam O'Meara, John Smurthwaite and Colin Smythe. Additionally, the researches of Terry Moylan, Andrew Carpenter and Robert Hogan, and the many suggestions of Roy Clements, bibliophile extraordinaire, have been invaluable. Thank you too, as always, to our families.

Index of Titles and First Lines

First lines are given in italics.